Takashi Nagai

Biography

The Narrative of an Atomic Bomb Survivor

CONTENT

1. Calmness, the Number One Son

2. Kublai Khan, Tsune and Pascal

3. The Mouse Who Could Not See the Stars

4. The Hidden Christians

5. Silent Night and a Precious Life

6. The Great Pan Is Dead

7. The Machine That Turned on Its Master

8. But Midori Will Be beside Me

9. When the Sun Turned Black

10. And the Rain Turned to Poison

11. The Last Black Hole in the Universe?

12. High Noon, and a Nation Wept

13. Not from Chance Our Comfort Springs

14. The Little Girl Who Could Not Cry

15. The Song of a Tokyo Leper

16. The Navel of the World

17. Cherry Blossoms Fall on the Third Day

18. For All That Has Been, Thanks; for All That Will Be, Yes

Calmness, the Number One Son

The historic and pristine Shimane Prefecture is where Takashi Nagai first came into being. The Sea of Japan washes along its extensive shoreline, which is northeast by north of Hiroshima. In the northwest, Siberia's mountain valleys are covered in snowdrifts during the winter months by the howling winds. If you look at a map, you can see how ideal it was for the ancient Chinese and Korean settlers who came in response to the cry to "go east, young man, go east" since it was full of adventure and ideal. The sparsely populated land's hilly terrain and, most importantly, its verdant splendor, which springs up like fountains from the rich volcanic soil, astonished the newcomers. According to geologists, Japan floated on the sea floor off the Asian mainland 60 million years ago, resembling an unlikely embryo. The seafloor gave way and the islands of Japan sprang out of their dark womb as the tectonic plates beneath the Pacific Ocean and the East Asian continent shifted ponderously into one another.

The "Ring of Fire"—the earthquake-volcano arc that extends up the west coast of South America, through Mexico and California, across the Pacific to Hawaii and Japan, and south through Indonesia to New Zealand—is what old geography textbooks referred to as Japan. Volcanoes erupted everywhere as Japan emerged from the sea, spewing out volumes of lava that eventually cooled to become basalt rock. This basalt was crushed by glaciers that flowed gently down mountains during the ice ages, creating new valleys. The gradual process of forming Japan's lush valleys and fertile soil was carried out by wind, storms, and particularly cyclones that originated in the tropics.

Neolithic signs of human presence in Japan are discovered by historians. A cultural leap forward occurred in Japan around the time of Caesar's invasion of Britain, which coincided with the birth of Christ's grandparents. A few centuries later, a single clan established effective dominance and established a capital in the southern part of what is now Nara Prefecture.

The people had developed a rich Shinto mythology even before writing. Many of the semidivine actions of the Shinto heroes and heroines were performed in the vicinity of Shimane's Izumo Taisha shrine. Little Japanese youngsters continue to love the stories. For example, the terrible eight-headed monster that frightened the entire region until a brave god fought it fiercely and defeated it. In Nagai's elementary school, Shimane was revered as sacred territory since it was the cradle of the Nihon-teki (purely Japanese) spirit.

Nagai was born in Shimane Prefecture, south of the city of Izumo, and ten minutes' drive from Mitoya. It is a hamlet of a dozen cottages, some thatched with miscanthus reed, and is completely tucked away between low mountains. Thirty years ago, such thatched buildings were commonplace in rural Japan and are prime examples of folk art. In addition to blending in wonderfully with the rice fields, the thick thatch keeps buildings warmer in the winter and cooler in the summer. However, most thatched roofs have been rendered obsolete due to the high cost of renewing thatch, and the days of leisurely folk crafts are long gone. Takashi Nagai's relative Saburo Yasuda has preserved the house in its original condition from when Nagai was a youngster.

Near the house are the graves of Nagai's parents and grandparents. Their Shinto tombstones are made of natural, uncut stone, as opposed to the neatly cut granite found in Japan's primarily Buddhist cemeteries. Because of Shinto's reverence for nature, everything is preserved as much as possible. Although the father and grandfather now rest in peace together, the family's history is filled with violent incidents! Grandfather Fumitaka Nagai, who was descended from samurai, was an expert in kampo yaku, or Chinese herbal medicine, a practice that has a long history in both China and Japan. He was given the title of doctor and began working in Tai, which translates to "the well in the rice fields."

The name Noboru, which translates to "calmness," was that of Grandfather Fumitaka's "Number One Son" (firstborn son). He was anything but! He was expelled from all six of the schools where his father tried him because of his erratic behavior. Dr. Nagai recruited a private teacher out of despair and at great financial expense. With the help of headmasters, deputies, and strict procedures, his son had been able to demoralize instructors in six different schools. Now that he was up against just one teacher, he eagerly applied his not-too-insignificant skills to the task. The instructor quickly changed her mind and revealed a spotless pair of heels. Fumitaka, which translates to "elegant nobility," was a patient guy from the traditional East.

Was the hyperactive rebelliousness subdued by the intense daily grind of working between cedar and cypress rows up the steep slope and on paddy terraces? Noboru started to observe the morning and evening skies, the fertile soil, and the dependability of the mountains as he worked by himself in an unfamiliar quiet. Among the astonishments of life in the open, he found satisfaction in unexpected storms that soaked him. Slowly, like snowdrifts before early spring breezes, his skepticism melted. Gradually, a determination became stronger until he packed his little possessions and vanished in his twenties. The young Japanese man set out with his father in mind, just like the prodigal son in the Bible. He had a duty to uphold his father's name, home, and occupation as the eldest son. Now he was consumed by guilt and resolved to make things right.

He made a lot of trips before he was hired as a general assistant by a doctor who practiced the latest Western medicine. All day long, he stood by the doctor's side while he operated or treated patients, mixed his prescriptions, saw new patients, and took messages. He would spend his nights poring over the medical texts that the good doctor had provided him. His mind had always been flawless, and his physique was strong and resilient from working the land in all kinds of weather and eating wholesome rural food.

With the noose beneath his chin, little Noboru would tie a rope from the rafters and diligently study till the wee hours of the morning. He woke up with a jerk whenever he fell asleep! With the farmer's fists clenched, the doctor offered his assistant every chance to read medical texts and help patients. Over time, those rough hands grew softer and more skilled at feeling for anomalies in stomachs and duplicating medical schematics. The boy who detested studying grew up to be an avid reader. He grew to love the idea of putting his hands and intellect up against death and illness, our ancient foes.

At the age of twenty-five, he felt prepared to take the Meiji government's Ministry of Health exams, which he passed with flying colors. It was 1904. His passport to return to his father's home was the parchment medical degree. In keeping with his moniker, Elegant Nobility, the father greeted his son with open arms. He had never given up on Noboru, and he had bowed to the East every morning at daybreak in his garden. He thanked all the gods and the sun for his favors and then pleaded with them to assist Noboru in taking responsibility. He begged them to take him home one day every night.

Since the time of Confucius, five hundred years before the time of Christ, filial piety has been a fundamental aspect of Far Eastern life. It was the most important virtue in Shimane, a culture that valued tradition. The father's cup was nearly full now. He watched with pride for three years while his son worked diligently and successfully at the nearby hospital to rebuild his reputation. It was time to locate a wife for Noboru.

The intermediary who brought Dr. Noboru and the qualified Tsune—which translates to "constant"—together was aware of his intentions. Tsune's lively disposition complemented that of the self-made and vivacious Dr. Noboru, and she was from an old samurai family. Once, when Tsune was still a single adolescent, a burglar stole into her house and sneaked into the room where she slept by herself. He covered her mouth with his palm, brandished a knife, and warned her of the consequences if she shouted. She nodded, and he was comforted by her poise. "Lead me to money," he said. "Yes, but first I just must go to the bathroom," she remarked, getting to her feet and bowing. She slid out after making another bow. A moment of confusion, and then he came at her, whispering threats, knife in hand. Running into the bathroom, she hurled the wooden bolt home. He had not anticipated this situation! She reappeared, bowed, slid back to her chamber without a word, and guided him to a money box. She bowed and gave it to him after hastily counting it and acknowledging that it was all she had. He was caught up by the police the following day. They only needed to look for cash with lipstick on it after narrowing down their suspect list based on her description. She had applied this novel cosmetic on her lips and then to her fingers in the restroom.

The next year, Tsune was experiencing labor pains while the young physician was on a sick call. The situation became urgent as the spasms reached their peak. The pregnant mother's face was covered in oily perspiration, and the baby's head refused to come out. "I'll have to crush the baby's head," the attending physician finally stated. Her voice was low and dry from the agony and anxiety, but her determination was unmistakable. "No. Don't murder my child.

A few hours later, Tsune's husband came home to be met by a tearful, red-faced son. The size of the head caught the doctor's attention right away. That big, nearly smashed head would eventually make a lot of people chuckle in hatter's stores. When the young parents used one of the ideographs from his own name to call the boy Takashi, which means "nobility," the elderly herbalist grandfather was extremely moved. When he joined the young couple in the Shinto shrine's Thanksgiving ceremony, his cup was full.

Deeply rooted in Confucian filial piety, he viewed himself as the heir to the hopes and trust of innumerable ancestors whose bravery and selflessness had given him life and a name, rather than as an individual. When his own Number One Son, Noboru, appeared insensitive to that trust, he had suffered greatly. Everything was fixed now. At just sixty-one, he passed away shortly after the baby's Thanksgiving ceremony, but he was a happy man. It was 1910.

Noboru was devastated by the unexpected passing of a father who had endured so much because of him. He knew his father appreciated formal obsequies, so the young doctor set them up. The lofty jet-black headdress worn by the Shinto Kannushi was the same as that of the Emperor's court in the sixth century a.d., and they wore white linen kimonos. Noboru's heart was numb, yet the antique woodwinds' melancholy sounds spoke to it. He believed that their songs were undoubtedly derived from the snow crane and the untamed geese of the marshes and moors of those prehistoric days when Japan was still known as Yamato.

Kublai Khan, Tsune and Pascal

Looking like a German university student, Nagai felt comfortable wearing the stark black uniform with brass buttons. Meiji When planning its massive advance in the 1870s, Japan chose the Western countries that seemed to offer the finest options. It adopted the British navy model and the Prussian educational model. Germans and Japanese have many traits, such as meticulous, systematic, and organized methods. Young Nagai would be studying medical texts written in German and using German medical techniques since the Japanese were drawn to the accuracy and completeness of German medical treatment.

The Nagasaki Medical University was a collection of white structures made of reinforced concrete. Part of the expanding northern suburbs, it was located at the base of Mount Konpira, which rose to a height of 1,200 feet. Beyond there, towering 1,089 feet like the counterpoise of Mount Konpira, was the green grandeur of Mount Inasa. To the southwest lay the glittering Nagasaki Bay. The huge red-brick cathedral, which could hold 5,000 worshippers, was located a third of a mile north of the university. He was shocked and annoyed by its size as well as by its penetrating bells, which chimed the Angelus three times a day. Japan was abandoning religious superstition and entering the age of enlightenment. The belief in Shinto's insufficient gods was already a terrible thing for modern Japanese, but he found it offensive that people would sacrifice their knowledge to foreign deities. He had no idea how the Urakami Cathedral would eventually affect his life.

April marks the start of studies at Japanese colleges and universities, and Nagai was enchanted by the diversity and hue of flowers that welcomed spring in the semitropical Nagasaki. During one of the first lectures, a professor showed Nagai's class a body and said,

"Gentlemen, this is man, the object of our studies." a bodily body. You can observe, weigh, test, and measure things. And man is only this. This rejection of the spiritual did not seem strange to Nagai.

Saying he had no beliefs would be inaccurate. He had a strong belief in science and was certain that it was the answer to all the problems preventing human advancement. His faith inspired him to pursue his studies with the same zeal his father had displayed three decades prior. Nagai also had faith in "humanity." The long Dark Ages had been overtaken by science, and humanity was finally emerging from its shadows. Banzai for the human race's amazing future!

At last, he had faith in Japan. He got a sense of the breadth and depth of Japanese history and culture from his growing understanding of the classics. The Manyoshu, a compilation of over 4,500 poems, the most of which were composed in the latter half of the seventh and the early part of the eighth centuries A.D., was read by him with pleasure and increasing amazement. The Manyoshu is a remarkable literary work by any country's standards. The poetry are poetic, new, and Nihon-teki, or authentically Japanese. One The modest status of many of the Manyoshu contributors enhances and even makes this book special.

Nagai, a young student, was beginning to view the Manyoshu as a sort of sacred writ. Throughout his life, the Manyoshu and several other types of traditional Japanese poetry had such a strong effect and were frequently included in his writing that a non-Japanese reader might benefit from a few examples.

The majority of Manyoshu's poetry is very sentimental. Soldierly devotion is demonstrated by a Manyoshu warrior who says, "If we die for you, O Emperor, we die without regret, whether we fall and rot in grass on the mountainside or perish as bloated corpses in the sea." A sophisticated love of nature can be seen in several Manyoshu poetry, such as "The moon, like a boat, sails through the forest of stars and the cloud-waves stir on the sea of heaven." Romantic love is a common motif in Manyoshu: a warrior writes to his lady, "I will hazard a double-edged sword and die content if it be for your sake." "As if to say, 'Good, go ahead and die of love!' that cruel girl passes right by the gate of my house," is an example of sardonic humor that occasionally appears. Poetry in Japanese doesn't rhyme. With a set number of syllables, the literary form is austere yet able to convey a wide range of emotions.

Shortly after enrolling at Nagasaki Medical University, Nagai became a member of a poetry club that was started by renowned poet Professor Mokichi Saito of the medical school. In Japan, it is not unusual for a seamstress, admiral, politician, or scientist to be a skilled poet as well.

In April 1928, Nagai enrolled at Nagasaki University. That was one year after the big bank crisis in Japan sent shock waves across the land, reaching even the peaceful valley of his parents. By 1929, the Depression was engulfing the entire world. Japanese industry had been growing rapidly, but in a few disastrous years, the West threatened to destroy her export-dependent economy by imposing massive taxes on Japanese exports, up to 50%. Farmers were severely impacted by the decline in silk prices. An increasing number of his rural patients would stoop down and request that Dr. Nagai or his spouse postpone their payments for a bit longer. The doctor took a job at a hospital a few miles away to make ends meet.

At Nagasaki Medical University, Dr. Noboru Nagai and his spouse resisted letting their son's life be disrupted by the deepening Depression. Although his stipend was not princely, they paid it to him every month, supporting his growing interest in Japanese poetry and asking him to focus solely on his studies. As a result of the latter, he became increasingly interested in studying Japanese history and culture and became more proud of his race.

He spent a portion of one holiday exploring the port of Hakata, which is located next to Fukuoka. He had read much about the thirteenth-century siege of Hakata and wanted to see the seven-hundred-year-old ruins and walk over the ground made sacred by the do-or-die battles against the vaunted warriors of Kublai Khan. In 1264, this Mongol emperor—the grandson of Genghis Khan—established the Yuan dynasty in Beijing. The Mongols had, since grandfather Genghis' time, swept all before them—central Asia, southern Russia and much of the Near East. Every army opposing them in Silesia, Hungary, and even as far as the Adriatic Sea had been routed by the renowned Mongolian horsemen. Kublai, Genghis Khan's grandson, was a formidable conqueror and was considered one of the greatest generals of all time. Sensing that his reputation would scare the Japanese, Kublai Khan dispatched envoys to demand that they acknowledge his suzerainty.

The Japanese gave his delegation short shrift. Enraged by this insult, he assembled a formidable invasion force in Korea, requisitioning Chinese and Korean ships to cross the narrow straits to Hakata Bay, 125 miles east. Soon after, the Mongols landed in Hakata and took control of the Japanese islands off the coast. However, the weather turned foul and a cyclone threatened. The Mongol general, fearing the destruction of his fleet in the exposed bay, decided to head back to Korea and return when the weather was good. The Japanese had fought tenaciously, but now the Mongols knew the lay of the harbor and land and were confident of crushing the small samurai force the next time.

Japan was frantically preparing for the next attack. Shinto shrines, Buddhist temples, the imperial court in Kyoto, and the military dictatorship in Kamakura all participated in a nationwide prayer campaign. All throughout the country, the same message was spread: Japan is a gift from the gods to the Emperor and his people. It must be treated as a holy trust, and the greatest honor anyone could hope for would be to die protecting it against the pagan Mongol hordes. To deter the feared Mongol cavalry, a ten-foot-tall wall was constructed around Hakata Bay.

The Mongols launched the largest seaborne invasion in history in June 1281, with 150,000 men on board Chinese and Korean vessels. The sluggish junks were hounded like enraged insects by small Japanese craft that flew at them as soon as the enemy fleet appeared on June 23. However, the offshore islands were swiftly captured by the Mongols, who then massacred every man. After methodically raping the women, they hung them alive from the ships' prows by piercing their wrists and running rope through them. That made the fate of the grim samurai's wives and daughters who waited on the beaches and sand dunes of Hakata Bay all too evident.

Signs that cheered Japanese hearts emerged in the southwestern sky on the evening of August 14. With a harsh cheer in every samurai's throat, a typhoon hit Hakata Bay the following day, August 15, smashing monstrous Mongol boats together or stacking them like matchwood on the northern peninsula. Before their wrath was over, the ferocious winds howled for two days. On August 17, a sight for weary Japanese eyes was presented by the calm and clear daybreak.

Full with hope for both his own and Japan's future, Nagai returned to the quiet classrooms and labs of his institution. He played basketball for the university and was doing well academically. He was finally able to play a game! He weighed 157 pounds and was five feet seven inches tall, which was large for a Japanese person. The cheerleading squad given him the endearing moniker "University Wall" because he played forward. That year, his squad placed third in the national tournaments and won the western Japan championship. He enjoyed being well-liked by the young nurses. He was unconcerned with the rising star of the militarists and showed little interest in politics. In the pubs along the docks, which were stocked with ladies of easy virtue, he was not unknown. He occasionally drank a lot of sake with his classmates, becoming somewhat famous for being able to hold more sake than anybody else in his class.

Like a sea captain enjoying the tang of the ocean, he inhaled the carbolic-tinged2 air as he strolled through the university hospital. He did feel like a captain-in-training, indeed. After completing two years of school, he would be Dr. Nagai in just two more years, bowed to by patients and nurses as he passed down these hallways with a stethoscope. He would be in charge of people's lives; his choices and knowledge would truly save their lives! Japan's life expectancy remained significantly lower than that of Western nations.

Shortly after classes began, his father sent him a troubling telegram. The words were direct: "Come home." He tossed in the inevitable books and packed hastily and nervously. He pondered anxiously about his mother while he sat in the northbound train and gazed out the window. He had tried to get more information from her throughout the recent holidays after seeing a certain slowing down. She changed the topic, laughed, and made fun of him for looking for a patient to practice on. The idea that anything could go wrong with this woman, who played such a significant role in his life, made him nervous.

At their house's genkan, or porch, his father greeted him. When Takashi found out that his mother had had a stroke and was unable to talk, he was shocked. She was pretty low but conscious. Her eyes followed him pitifully as he walked to her side, and she knew that he was her Number One Son. On tatami, the thick straw matting that covers most Japanese floors, she laid on a futon, or quilt. He took her hand and sat next to her without shoes. She was unable to express herself, but he could see her feelings clearly reflected in the almond-shaped, dark eyes that met his. It appeared to him that she had postponed the last stages of her brain hemorrhage until she was ready to bid him farewell. Minutes later, she passed away. Later, he wrote: "I rushed to her bedside." The encounter would transform his life. She continued to breathe. The end resulted from the way she stared at me. In one final, piercing look, my mother destroyed the ideological foundation I had built. I could hear it plainly from the woman who had given birth to me, raised me, and never once wavered in her love for me—even in her final moments! "Your mother now takes leave in death, but her living spirit will be beside her little one, Takashi," she said, her eyes meeting me with finality. When I was told that there was no such thing as a spirit, I couldn't help but believe it! I learned from my mother's eyes that people's spirits continue to exist after they pass away. All of this was the result of an intuition that was based on conviction. An essential term in Japanese is chokkan, which means "intuition." Choku, which means "immediate" or "direct," and Kan, which means "feelings"—that is, something that comes straight to the feelings—are the two ideographs that make up this phrase. Far Easterners hold this information in the highest regard.

The physical sciences provided Nagai with what appeared to be the only trustworthy paths to truth since his senior year of high school. This nonscientific "intuition" that his mother's ghost was still alive perplexed him. Was this a genuine, unquestionable instance of satori, or enlightenment, which the Zen people described as "the flash of a sword cutting through the problems of existence"? Or was his keen perception only an unconscious ploy brought on by emotional wishful thinking? Though he wasn't positive, the encounter made him reconsider the lengthy history of "wisdom" thinkers in China and Japan. He pointed out that many of the ancient ideographs he read every day firmly affirmed their belief that a person's heart is superior to his mind.

Nagai had been moved by a line from Blaise Pascal's Pensées during a literary class in high school. "Man is a thinking reed," the Frenchman from the seventeenth century wrote. The sentence sounded Japanese, as if it were uttered by a Buddhist priest. After elaborating on Pascal's literary style as the model for contemporary French prose, the instructor came to the conclusion that Pascal was that intriguing kind of person—a poet-scientist. When Nagai heard that, he felt a stir. He encountered Pascal once more as the syringe's inventor while pursuing his medical education at Nagasaki University.

In order to allow himself more time to process his mother's passing, a distraught Nagai decided to take a boat part of the way to Nagasaki after her funeral. Over a gloomy and turbulent sea, gray clouds scudded low, suggesting that nature sympathized with his loss. He pulled out his copy of the Pensées and started reading while he was alone on the deck of the ship heading south. This marked the beginning of a new journey.

The Mouse Who Could Not See the Stars

There isn't much about science in The Pensées. It functions as a sort of journal of Pascal's quest for philosophical truths. Words like "grace," "paradise lost," and "redemption" left Nagai mostly perplexed. He was perplexed by strange biblical quotes as well as a variety of Western analogies and historical references. However, there were several passages that resonated with Nagai and gave him hope that Pascal might have a very significant vision.

The highest authority granted to human reason at Nagasaki University was not acknowledged by Pascal. Remorselessly, the Frenchman mocked anyone who would depend solely on human reason. At night, we dream and construct a fantasy world. How does reason know that we are not experiencing identical illusions in our current waking state? Nagai was aware that some of the greatest Eastern religious philosophers believed that human philosophy was "a dream about a dream" and that the "reality" outside of us was only an illusion.

Pascal identified two erroneous attitudes toward reason. One is an overconfidence in reason, which frequently results in skepticism that is devoid of substance. The other is acceptance of foolishness resulting from indolence or apathy. Avoiding these two traps leads to truth. It takes effort, but if you don't want to do the hunt, you're a "deserter." The Frenchman went on to say that human reason can only arrive at lower scientific facts, not the ultimate objective reality. The greater truths, which are of the order of wisdom and are received rather than understood, are far more significant than simple scientific facts. The greater realities are perceived "by the eyes of the heart," in contrast to the logical truths of science. Buddhism had taught Nagai that expression. The eye of the heart, which sees beyond outward appearances, is symbolized by the jewel in the forehead of many

Buddha pictures. Buddhism's Hanya, or Wisdom, sutra reflected Pascal's reliance on a higher order than reason. The Frenchman went on to say that "the heart has reasons of which reason knows nothing."

Nagai set the book down and listened to the ship's gulls' wailing lament. After realizing he was hungry, he pulled out his lunchbox, or o-bento, and started eating skillfully with chopsticks. He was uneasy in the Pensées. Why? Because the Far Eastern way of thought was completely different from it? Of all Western philosophy and religion, many Japanese people said that. When traveling with his father, he recalled the first time he sat down to a Western breakfast in a restaurant. He did not enjoy the lunch since he felt so awkward using a knife and fork. He felt disappointed since there was no rice, which is a necessary component of a Japanese breakfast, nor was there bean paste soup or seaweed flakes. He did, however, like a quick Western breakfast because he was accustomed to eating Western cuisine. Could it be that he needed to stay with Pascal a bit longer?

He walked down the deck after putting away his lunchbox. Pascal used reason to support his claim that reason was not the highest faculty. That was a vicious circle, wasn't it? According to Pascal, the secrets of God and life cannot be understood by unaided human reason. However, when an honest believer prays, God does disclose the fundamental facts. "Faith is a gift of God.... You must pray for it," Pascal concluded. Nagai leaned against the railing of the deck and gazed blankly at the horizon, wondering: If I don't believe in God, how can I pray honestly? This is undoubtedly where the Frenchman's logic breaks down, since praying is a sign of a blind faith in God's existence and a surrender of reason and intellectual accountability!

Nagai adopted a different approach: If God existed, he would undoubtedly make his presence more apparent to us if he cared about us as much as Pascal asserted. Or was that kind of reasoning childish? Pascal asserted that religion was founded on an individual's inner experience of God and that "there is enough light for those who desire only to see and enough darkness for those of a contrary disposition." Nagai contrasted this assertion with his personal belief that his mother's spirit lived on after her physical passing. Did that come from some rudimentary protective instinct against the despair that may overtake one at the death of a loved one, or was that a real experience?

He resumed playing the Pensées. Pascal brought to light a conflict in both human history and the consciousness of all serious thinkers. We are both magnificent and miserable. "We are as miserable as dispossessed kings." Pascal penned the statement with a sense of familiarity, stirring Nagai with the prospect of a vast universe of timeless beauty and meaning. The old saying, "A mouse cannot see the stars, nor an earthworm the flowers," came to Nagai's sorrowful mind.

The teacher's remarks regarding Marx's statement that "Religion is the opium of the people" came back to him: "Lads, the Chinese opium poppy is beautiful, and so is much in the religions of the world." However, religion has the power to transport you to a deadly dreamworld, where you think a Buddha or god would suddenly save the day.

Nagai turned back to Pascal. "Christ has been a haven for some and a roadblock for others—the Christian faith has always endured, but it has always been attacked." Indeed, Christianity was viewed by the Tokugawa shoguns as an alien force that needed to be eradicated from Japan. In the 1600s, tens of thousands of Japanese Christians had perished. Japanese Christians were characterized as traitors to the kokutai, the distinctive national polity, by the Tokugawa tyrants and, more recently, the militarists. Nagai's fervent devotion to the kokutai heightened some of the unease he had while reading some of Pensées's severe passages. To his beloved Nihon, they appeared so alien and un-Japanese.

Nagai devoted himself fully to his medical studies after returning to Nagasaki, but the issues brought on by his mother's passing persisted. Even if there are many indications of male dominance in Japan, many social scientists still view the country as a "mother society." In Japanese culture, the mother is the dominant, yet occasionally inconspicuous, figure. Nagai now understood that the person who had shaped him the most had not been his strict and well-respected father, but rather his kind mother. He wished he could talk to her about his new spiritual issues, but it was too late.

Friends from university saw a shift in Nagai. His naive optimism and blind faith in science as a means of deliverance and in the promise of utopia were gone. He started to criticize his lecturers more. One of them enthusiastically described human mental functions, such as thoughts and emotions, in terms of electric currents flowing through the brain shortly after his mother's dying. When Nagai asked for specifics, the professor was unable to provide them, acknowledging that it was only a theory. Nagai compiled a list of insightful theories he had come across in medical textbooks that had been modified or dropped in subsequent iterations. He yearned to discover "absolute truth," as Pascal put it. Was Pascal merely whistling in the dark, or was there something like that?

He had been limited to lectures, lab work, animal dissection, and finally corpse dissection for the preceding two years. In his third year, he started going around the hospital wards with doctor-professors to examine patients. He became aware that his mother's passing had made him more empathetic after observing how certain doctors' icy demeanors may harm and even demoralize patients. He continued to enjoy drinking sessions with pals, play basketball, and occasionally climb mountains. He believed that he now understood the words of poets such as the seventeenth-century Basho: "Great beauty is all around you; you don't have to travel to a far country to see it." He was starting to grasp what Zen masters refer to as the "suchness" in a plover's cries on a desolate beach, in a bowl of cheap green tea, or in a typical garden-variety blossom. But his heart was not at rest, and he summed up this time in his life in a book he authored fifteen years later: "I was deeply troubled for five years by a little voice I heard, waking and sleeping: 'What is the meaning of our lives?'" In my search for the purpose of my existence, I read the biographies of a wide range of people, but the more I read, the more complicated the issue became. It did, of course; I was researching other people's lives, not mine. They do not own my life. Every one of us has a distinct life with a distinct meaning.

Before factory machines made women's apparel cheap and identical, you undoubtedly recall the exquisite lace that ladies created in their homes.

The Hidden Christians

The Christian origins of Sadakichi Moriyama date back three centuries, to the period when Nagasaki was the only Christian city in Japan. The first time the Japanese heard the Christian gospel was when Saint Francis Xavier arrived in Kagoshima on August 15, 1549. There was no Japanese-European dictionary, and no European had yet ventured inland. As a result, Xavier started preaching Dai Nichi, which caused him a lot of issues. To his dismay, Xavier discovered that Dai Nichi was a Buddha manifestation rather than the Japanese name for the Almighty God of the Bible. But faith is more often caught than taught, and the vivacious Basque aristocrat so captivated many Japanese that they requested baptism.

The history of Catholic missions throughout the colonial era contains several chapters that are unsettling to read. Among these is the narrative of the Jesuits in Japan. Due to their strong personalities, strong beliefs, and efforts to help the sick, destitute, and orphaned, the men who followed Xavier gained a lot of followers from both the aristocracy and the general populace. For example, sculptures of the Jesuit surgeon Luis de Almeida, who invented surgery in Japan, have been placed by civic authorities in Japan. When Dr. Almeida joined the Jesuits, he was already a successful investor in the Far East. He made arrangements for his possessions to be invested in the profitable Macao-Japan silk trade prior to taking his vows, with the condition that all profits be sent to Japanese Jesuit hospitals and orphanages.

Arriving as the Jesuit mission's superior in 1579, Alessandro Valignano was to prove to be just as successful as Xavier. A giant in body and mind, he had been educated in the secular Renaissance and practiced law before entering the Jesuit order at the age of twenty-seven. By immersing himself in Saint Ignatius' Spiritual Exercises, he improved his prayer and even his contemplative skills and was promoted to novice master.

Centuries before his time, Valignano became a missionary. In a brief summary of the perils of colonialism today, he urged his men to study and appreciate the language and culture of the people they served. He did not allow Western cultural burdens to be placed on Asian shoulders. Instead of teaching Spanish, Portuguese, or Italian culture, Jesuits traveled to the East to spread the gospel. Do not associate the Gospel with European civilization of the sixteenth century, but by all means share Western astronomy, medicine, and science with the Eastern people. To the dismay of some, he implied that Europeans were only better than Japanese in their understanding of the Gospels and pushed that his troops train Japanese to assume leadership roles.

Many Japanese feudal barons, known as daimyo, converted to Christianity or showed a strong regard for the new faith. Ukon Takayama, also known as "the Japanese Thomas More," was one of them. He was one of the most important political and cultural personalities of his time, much like the former chancellor of England. Takayama's refusal to compromise his Christian beliefs led to his incarceration and the loss of his castle and holdings. Just as Henry VIII sought to win Chancellor More, dictator Hideyoshi made a concerted effort to win this exceptional military tactician, calligrapher, and tea ceremony expert over to his cause. Takayama's refusal to give up his Christian beliefs ultimately led to his deportation from Japan.

Tens of thousands of peasants and townspeople, as well as a large number of samurai, requested baptism. When persons like Takayama started referring to Christ as their Shukun, or leige ruler, who was given complete obedience to no other ruler, dictator Hideyoshi became concerned about the rapid growth of Christians. Wasn't the samurai code under danger because of this? At first, the dictator had supported Christianity because he was captivated by the Jesuits and their wealth of Western knowledge. He suddenly outlawed Christianity during one of his infamous mood episodes. Foreign missionaries were forced to leave Japan, and all Japanese Christians were forced to renounce their faith. In order to make his point, he had 26 Christians arrested in Kyoto, the capital city, and forced to march for 30 days on foot through the bitter cold to Nagasaki. Upon their arrival, they were to be crucified.

Nagasaki was a purposeful choice. Before it became the main port for the European ships carrying the new and thriving trade between China (via Macao) and Japan in 1571, Nagasaki was not a significant town. Baron Omura was a Christian daimyo who owned the port. Buddhist monks had previously received land grants from daimyo for monasteries and schools.

When the 26 barefoot, travel-weary victims hobbled into Nagasaki, the Moriyamas were Christians. A man who had little faith, dictator Hideyoshi believed that a public display of bloodshed would soon persuade Christians in Nagasaki to give up their beliefs. He therefore mandated that the executions be slow public performances. When the condemned were announced to arrive in Nagasaki, a large crowd of Christians gathered to applaud and yell encouragement. Near the current Nagasaki train station, the 26 were marched to Nishizaka Hill. To ensure that everyone could enjoy the spectacle, twenty-six carefully cut crosses ran from the hill's brow down toward the harbor. Straw ropes and iron rings were used to secure the victims to the crosses. Each cross had two samurai waiting to run their swords up under the inmates' rib cages, each holding an unsheathed bamboo lance. To increase the fear of the condemned and bystanders, this last act was postponed.

The line of crosses began to sing, "Praise the Lord, ye children of the Lord," and the audience halted to listen as the commotion over the hillside subsided. All Japanese Christian groups regularly chanted the Sanctus, which is the portion of the Latin Mass that comes before the consecration, after the psalm ended. He was becoming nervous because it was turning into a demonstration of Christian power instead of the gory exhibition that Dictator Hideyoshi had demanded.

Among the twenty-six, one requested permission to speak. He was the thirty-three-year-old Jesuit Paul Miki, a successful preacher and catechist, and the son of a commander in Baron Takayama's army. Samurai placed a great deal of importance on dying well, and they frequently sang a jisei no uta, or farewell song, as they passed away. "I am Japanese and a brother of the Society of Jesus," Miki said in a powerful voice that echoed to the outskirts of the gathering. I haven't done anything wrong. I have only been sentenced to death because I have preached the gospel of our Lord Jesus Christ. I accept death as a wonderful gift from my Lord and am glad to die for it. Miki asked the audience whether they could see the 26 people's faces showing fear. He reassured them that since heaven existed, they shouldn't be afraid.

Following the death of dictator Hideyoshi, the feudal barons engaged in a fierce power battle. After winning, Ieyasu Tokugawa assumed the title of shogun and became a more totalitarian tyrant than Hideyoshi. The first Tokugawa ruler harbored a strong mistrust of Christianity, particularly Catholicism. He was troubled by the fact that aristocracy like Baron Takayama and common peasants defied the all-powerful Hideyoshi in favor of this forbidden alien faith, and he observed missionaries traveling with the conquistadors on colonial expeditions all across the world. After eliminating any remaining opposition to his reign, the shogun reinstated the ban on Christianity in 1614.

The group who traveled north of Nagasaki to a rugged area of the countryside where the tiny Urakami River flowed into Nagasaki Bay included Sadakichi Moriyama's ancestors. They established an underground church and became become farmers and fishermen. They designated a chokata, or "head man," as the general leader; a "water man" to perform baptisms; and a "calendar man" to maintain the dates of Advent, Christmas, Lent, Easter, and so on. The first Chokata were Sadakichi Moriyama's forefathers, and each eldest son took on the role after his father passed away. By establishing a police state, the Tokugawa shoguns were able to maintain their hold on power for two and a half centuries, and their steadfast antagonism to Christianity never wavered. The seventh member of the Chokata line, Kichizo Moriyama, was caught in a police trap in 1856. Despite being tortured to death, he never betrayed his confidence. Sadakichi Moriyama was to be fathered by his baby son.

Japan signed a commercial contract with the United States in 1858 after being compelled to open up to the outside world by Commodore Perry's gunboats. Soon after, Europeans arrived in Japan and settled in cities like Nagasaki and Yokohama. The shogun declared that only Europeans might enter the chapels they were starting to construct. For the Japanese, Christianity was forbidden. Just below the current Glover Mansion of Madam Butterfly renown, in the southern Nagasaki district of Oura, Father Petitjean of the Paris Foreign Mission Society finished a church in February 1864.

The hidden Christian hamlet of Urakami was located four miles down the bay from this church. The pro tem Christian leaders were very hesitant to act swiftly because, only six years prior, they had witnessed their chokata hauled away to die brutally in prison. They further contended that the new Christian Church might not be their forebears'.

One market day, a group of Urakami Christians passed the new Oura church. One of them managed to enter the building without being noticed and saw a statue of Mary cradling the Christ child. When they asked locals about the tall, black-clad Frenchman, they were informed that he had no wife. Outside the church, they also noticed the menacing government notice board that said it was only for foreigners and that any Japanese found inside would face the full force of the anti-Christian laws.

Father Petitjean was reciting his breviary in a gloomy manner within the church. In the sixty years following Francis Xavier's initial baptisms, he had been captivated by literature on Japanese Christians while he was a seminarian in Paris. He had studied the in-depth stories of Lady Tama Hosokawa, Baron Ukon Takayama, the 26 people who were crucified at Nagasaki, and the thousands of Japanese people from all walks of life who decided to die rather than give up their Christian beliefs. He had arrived in Nagasaki with great expectations, hoping to find some remaining Christians when Japan opened to the West. To his dismay, he discovered only anti-Christian sentiment. He knelt in his new church by himself today, and the weather matched his attitude.

The group of raggedly dressed Japanese women from Urakami crossed the tatami floor to confront him, and he looked up sharply. A woman named Yuri, which translates to "lily," questioned, "Santa Maria no gozo wa doko?" "Where is the Holy Mary statue?" Too shocked, the priest could not respond.

Father Petitjean was informed that the Hidden Christians of Urakami met in the large cattle shed in Moriyama. He communicated with the elders, the calendar man, and the water man. He pretended to be a farmer and pursued darkness when they warned him of the danger if the city authorities found out who they were. With rice straw beneath his feet to conceal the filth, he conducted Mass in the cow shed.

Being sensitive to symbols, the Japanese were amazed that the first Mass was held in a cow shed. Throughout the 25 years of persecution, the tale of the small family's gloomy Advent and Christmas journeys—during which they were pursued by Herod's soldiers and denied refuge by the townspeople—remained a popular one. On December 25, they even fed the livestock more hay!

When Nagasaki authorities finally learned of the French priest and the covert Christians, they requested directives from the central government. Although with great uncertainty, the Tokugawa shogun continued to rule the country. The Tokugawa regime, which had virtually eradicated Japanese Christianity in the 1600s, ordered Nagasaki's civic authorities to put out these blazing Christian flames in this final year of its existence. Thus, on July 15, 1867, at 3 A.M., soldiers trudged through torrential rain and captured sixty-eight prominent Christians. Later, more were taken, and at last, all 3,414 Urakami Christians—from weak elderly people to screaming infants—were sent to 19 specially constructed prison facilities located around the country. To break their cohesiveness, the administration transported them to dispersed prison camps. Torture and the death penalty were to be applied if the Christians continued to practice their faith.

The Tokugawa government was ousted less than a year later, and Emperor Meiji took over as ruler. The new Meiji government placed a high premium on maintaining national unity in the face of hostile Western colonists advancing throughout Asia. Christianity was disruptive and Western. The Urakami Christians hobbled home just five years after being forcibly marched to faraway incarceration. Just under 20 percent, or 664 people, had perished in captivity, and many more were in bad physical condition. There had been an open season on their property since the government had declared them traitors. They had lost everything of value, including their boats, fishing gear, furnishings, and farming equipment. They were moved to tears by the untamed area that covered the once-tidy rice paddies.

Silent Night and a Precious Life

Professor Itsuma Suetsugu sat down glumly in a run-down office at Nagasaki Medical University at the same time that year, 1932. Last year, he had arrived at this university with the intention of establishing a radiology department. Gaining proficiency in this new area of medicine, which was still in its infancy even in Europe, had presented many challenges. Although Saint George's Hospital in Hamburg had been an excellent environment to study and work, Suetsugu had found it much more difficult because his research and studies had been conducted in German.

The professor believed he had planned for everything, but he had failed to account for the human element's unpredictability. Professional jealousy was an old demon that lurked in the hearts of many prominent professors at Nagasaki University, who gave eloquent lectures in their classrooms and seemed so committed to medicine and truth! Perhaps they were also afraid that their hard-won stethoscope art would become outdated due to Professor Suetsugu's new x-ray machine. The frigid reception he and his machine received left him speechless. It had been agreed that upon his return from Germany he would be provided with all he need for a separate department. However, he discovered that he and his gear were moved into some outdated rooms. Not even a restroom was present. He was casually instructed to use the restroom in the adjacent department. Additionally, the University Council would not permit him to erect the "Radiology Department" sign. The other teachers' vibrations were soon detected by the medical students. The students didn't spend much time on the assignments Dr. Suetsugu assigned them because they already had more than they wanted for the final exams. Another affront to Suetsugu was that radiology was not given much room in the exams; nonetheless, he got even by marking the papers. He handed a lot of his students what he believed was rightfully theirs—zero! Among those who had received a zero was Nagai.

It was late April now. While in the hospital recuperating, Nagai received a message from University Administration with a proposal that needed an immediate response. Nagai's right ear was severely deaf, therefore the visitor took the seat on the left. He leaned down and informed Nagai that stethoscope job would not be possible because to his persistent hearing impairment. The administration recommended that he work as Dr. Suetsugu's radiology assistant. Finally, the latter's grievances regarding radiology's utterly inadequate treatment had been taken into consideration. The administration had finally taken action after he refused to change his zero grades. Nagai was both cornered and shocked. The invitation to work at the university would be withdrawn if he declined. He replied he would take the offer even if he didn't think Suetsugu was a little strange.

The professor described his plans to Nagai a few weeks later, saying, "X-ray technology is the wave of the future." Japan must acknowledge that we are about forty years behind Europe in radiology. I'll be honest with you, Nagai. Medicine is already being revolutionized by X-ray technology, and it will continue to do so. Radiation exposure caused him to lose one finger, then another. At last, his right arm had to be amputated. Here is a copy of his notes on how to better shield medical professionals and technicians from radiation.

The notes were taken by Nagai. Even though he could read German, the text was nearly unreadable. "Oh, yes," the professor continued. It's challenging to read. He had to write with his left hand after the amputation. I have seen a stone monument in a Hamburg University garden that bears the names of at least a hundred persons who have perished as a result of radiation exposure from radiological research. Professors, physicians, nurses, technicians, and even a nun scientist are present. All of them are martyrs for the sake of scientific truth, giving their lives to save the lives of x-ray technology's patients worldwide. There are names from Poland, Germany, Belgium, Denmark, France, and England on that stone, but none from Japan. We must participate in this risky scientific endeavor until every big hospital, Nagai-kun, has a secure x-ray facility.

Suetsugu grew irritable. "We'll discover fresh facts that will last forever. Forever! Something is eternal if it is true. You would be working for ephemeral, frequently untrue goals if you become a politician. "Look at Genghis Khan's Mongols," he added solemnly, clearly referring to the militarists who were poised to take control of Japanese politics in that summer of 1932. They have no land to call their own today, despite having conquered parts of Europe and Asia. Tsuwamono domo no yume no ato, natsu kusa yo! The latter was a haiku poem written on a field where two enormous armies had engaged in combat. It was written by seventeenth-century Basho, one of Nagai's favorite poets.

As the first patient entered the dimly lit room, he now stood next to the professor. She was a pretty young lady with permanent waves in her hair, which was still unusual in Nagasaki. In order to demonstrate to Nagai that intestinal worms were the source of her discomfort, Suetsugu traced the barium fluid while speaking to him in German. Nagai pondered whether a young man was in love with her and whether seeing what they saw would lessen his admiration for her! The teacher who appeared tubercular was the following patient.

The middle of December 1932 was a very cold month. Despite the inadequately heated quarters, Nagai would often remain at the hospital after work, immersed in radiological study. He couldn't believe he had ever been so uninterested in the new science that Dr. Suetsugu had presented. Since it was December 24 and he had accepted the Moriyamas' invitation to join them for a special Christmas Eve lunch, he was leaving early tonight. Because it was "un-Japanese and alien," the militarists prohibited people from celebrating Christmas, and it was not a public holiday in Japan. Out of friendship and respect for his gracious hosts, Nagai would celebrate it tonight even though he had never done it before.

The tatami mat floor was just a foot above the Japanese-style dining table. Everybody sat in the traditional seiza position, with their feet flattened under their buttocks, their backs straight, and their insteps. "Dozo, O raku ni," stated host Moriyama. The men sat more comfortably, crossing their legs in front of them, after being asked to do so. The strict yet beautiful seiza style was never loosened by polite women. Midori, the sole child of the Moriyamas, was at home for the winter holidays on this specific night. Although Midori means "verdant," Nagai was instantly drawn to the raven-black hair that was incredibly shiny and luxurious, a testament to Midori's mother Tsumo, also known as "the Crow." Midori's mother's people, who had been outdoor dwellers since the early 1600s as Ukujima farmers and fishermen, were also responsible for her dark complexion and strong, flexible limbs. That night, Midori waited on them, and while she didn't say much, Nagai could see how pretty she was when she smiled. He had once been shown school album pictures of Midori as the middle blocker and sprint champion on the championship volleyball team by a proud Tsumo. In the beautiful flow of her movements, he saw an athletic girl.

The majority of the conversation was led by the father, who was soon glowing from hot sake and spoke passionately about his Christian forefathers during the persecutions. On Christmas nights, they would gather in what they called natara, the Moriyama cow shed. One example of the peculiar terms that had developed among these Hidden Christians—words that are not included in any Japanese dictionary—was natara. Although the terms were Latin or Portuguese in origin, three centuries of oral tradition had altered how they were pronounced. Their word for prayer, orassho, came from the Latin oratio. According to Moriyama, the shed and stalls would be cleaned before Christmas Eve, and meals would be prepared with hot water waiting on a charcoal stove. There would always be lookouts to provide the signal because police or government agents might be on the loose. In the event the police arrived to inquire about the situation, as was frequently the case under the brutal Tokugawa regime, the Christians turned into a group that paid respect to a deceased Moriyama in the manner of Buddhism. The elders' recitation of the tale of Mary and Joseph, who were turned away from lodging and wandered the cold night until they discovered a place to house farm animals, would be the night's high point. The story's retelling gave the Christians the strength to face another perilous year by making Christmas happen again. "We have our own problems with the police at the moment, but we have it much easier than our ancestors because we can celebrate midnight Mass in the cathedral tonight," Moriyama remarked.

The cowherd Moriyama leaned forward until his crimson face was near the doctor's after exchanging more hot sake with Nagai. "Why don't you accompany us to midnight Mass tonight, Sensei [Doctor]?" "Maybe God sent Nagai to us just for that," Moriyama said, encouraging his wife and Midori to pray for Nagai's conversion to Christianity ever since that Sunday when the obstinate student had asked for accommodation a second time. This had struck a chord with Midori.

At midnight Mass that night, around 5,000 people packed into the cathedral despite the snowfall. Even shabby farmers and laborers had dressed nicely, and the crowd was splattered with beautiful colors from the kimonos of women and girls. Every time they paused, Nagai was astounded by the silence and the might of the congregation's singing. Nagai knew the well-known Buddhist term and idea Mu. "A man burning a bundle over a fire" is the ideograph for Mu. It can be translated into English as "Emptiness," "the Void," or "No Thing." Buddhism maintains that since everything we own was given to us by someone else, we are all actually nothing and a blank. My parents, relatives, teachers, and ancestors all gave me gifts that have shaped my body, looks, language, and accent. Everything I use and every ounce of food I consume comes from other people. During the extended periods of silence, Nagai found himself reflecting on this age-old Asian idea.

His thoughts turned to another Buddhist idea that always fascinated and amused him: nature purposefully placed our navel in the exact spot where we view it every day when we take a bath. It was positioned there as a reminder that our bodies and every aspect of who we are are gifts. For nine solid months, we practically lived with our mother. As passive objects of her care and food, we did nothing at all to merit this. We are therefore genuinely mu, nothing, and the void in and of ourselves. However, there is another Mu. It is much beyond and beyond the "things" that our finite minds can comprehend, and it is not nothing but Nothing. Nagai questioned whether Pascal's "Absolute, Infinite God" and Buddhism's "No Thing" and "the Void" were interchangeable. "God is inexpressible, so the Bible is full of metaphors," he had read in the Pensées, and "our minds, like our senses, are very limited—too much light or too little light and we are blind; too much noise or too little noise and we are deaf." Pascal ended with a quote from the great Japanese Zen monk Dogen from the thirteenth century: "Even though we cannot understand the Truth with our limited reason, we can have a heart-experience of it." Nagai moaned to himself: reason was the only sure way for any guy to go. However, Dogen and Pascal argued that reason could never fully discover the Truth. Was this the religious believer's deadly blind spot? Did the fanaticism and wars that seemed to undermine the arguments of all the religions Nagai had read about stem from this tragic apparent rejection of reason? However, Pascal and Dogen seemed to have a generosity that ordinary "reasonable" individuals did not.

Nagai's slumber was cut short when the elderly priest climbed up on the pulpit. As the priest's reedy voice praised God's selection of a lowly carpenter and his virgin wife, 5,000 people fell silent. Our thoughts realize that this humility is the truth that will set us free. This is the deliverance that our hearts long for. Since the Holy Family embraced the anguish and darkness of this night because it was part of the Father's loving plan, how can we gripe about difficulties? The words made Nagai aware of all the materialism, greed, and sham in his heart, striking him like the blow a Zen master delivers to a slumbering apprentice!

Everyone stood to sing the Latin Credo as the priest stepped down from the platform. Nagai was not entirely unfamiliar with the words, which were used in Masses by the great composers. However, he was unnerved by tonight's Credo since Beethoven or Mozart's magnificent polyphony did not soften its uncompromising dogmatism. This Credo from 5,000 Urakami throats sounded more like a battle cry and a defiant roar. What had troubled him? Was it a reasonable response to "fanaticism," which was made more disturbing by the fact that it was presented in a highly un-Japanese manner? Or, he thought ruefully, was he troubled because he was a free-spirited scholar and ethical dilettante who was unable to take a straightforward position for kindness and truth, while others could?

Incense drifted over the altar lit by candles as the chanting ceased. Haru-gasumi, the delicate blue haze that hovers above Japanese mountains in the spring and is always suggestive of something endlessly tender, was what it reminded him of. The haru-gasumi was pierced by silvery bells, and everyone knelt once again. He was reminded of something deep within of him as he looked across the silence to the pinpoints of candlelight on the altar. He recalled going on a tramp over vast, silent mountains with a few friends during a university break. They would sit by the campfire's embers every night, frequently in solitude. Gazing up into the clear night sky, Nagai would select his favorite stars and listen to them like parts of an orchestra that only your kokoro, or heart, could hear. These candle glints, along with those constellations, alluded to a mysterious Beyond.

After the cathedral Mass ended, Nagai returned to his room in the Moriyamas' house. Even though he had been up for nearly twenty-four hours, he was still awake and comfortably nestled beneath a thick Japanese quilt. During the April Hata-age, the kite-flying festival, when hundreds of multicolored kites soared, plunged, and swerved as their operators tried to cut each other's strings, his mind was as restless as the skies over Nagasaki. Emotions and conflicting ideas fought against one another, driving sleep away. A scientist's innate mistrust of emotionalism contrasted with memories of the lavish medieval ceremony that took place that evening. Five thousand individuals, primarily from the working class, were moved by his faith to alternate between the ecstasy of Schubert's Ave Maria and the utmost quiet. However, his doctor's common sense alerted him to the fact that the most harmful and militant religions are those that emphasize strict discipline and binary solutions. I thought of Islam, Nichiren

Buddhism, and the Crusades. Voices from the past, instructors warning their students about the pathologic repercussions of autosuggestion, hysteria, and psychological manipulation, interrupted his recollection of his intuition of a loving Presence during the Mass. Pascal felt certain of the loving Presence at the Urakami Cathedral, although being aware of such risks. Pascal in Urakami? No, that was incorrect; it was Hamburg's Saint George's Cathedral. He made a mental scowl, but before he could correct it, fatigue overcame his thoughts and feelings, extinguishing his consciousness.

He worked in the radiology department as normal the following day, but he came home prepared for an early sleep. He was fast asleep before he had even changed into his nemaki and slithered beneath the fluffy futon. When Midori woke her parents at midnight with excruciating stomach pains, he was not aware of the movement underneath. Her mother suspected intestinal worms right away. Early in the 1930s, Japan had not yet reached completely hygienic standards. Only the wealthiest residences had sewage installed, and the farmers were impoverished and unable to purchase chemical fertilizer. Emptying toilet pit contents into farmlands and vegetable gardens was the solution to these two issues.

Sadakichi went upstairs and woke the young Dr. Nagai because it was snowing a lot and it would take a long time to get a doctor at that hour. Bowing and apologizing profusely, he described the issue. Without hesitation, Takashi diagnosed acute appendicitis. Midori has to be operated on right away. He looked away from Midori's bed to see Sadakichi light a candle while kneeling in front of a statue of the Virgin Mary. Takashi found it strange that poor Sadakichi said to no one in particular, "It's all God's will, and who knows what good will come from this."

Nagai rushed to adjacent Yamazato Primary School, being cautious not to trip over the snow, and instructed them to prepare Midori for transfer to the university hospital right away.

In this snowstorm, hailing a cab would take too long. We cannot afford to wait. Sadakichi's health had been deteriorating for a while. Tsumo was still out in a back room gathering the items she would need as tsukisoi to her daughter and the items Midori would require while she was in the hospital. Nagai referred to Sadakichi as "O-to-san," the title used by intimate friends and family. It sounds very personal but respectful and signifies "Dad." "I can easily handle Midori-san if you hold the lantern in front of me." Midori was so shocked that she lost all memory of her suffering. Be carried by a man through the streets? Who would notice us at this hour, she thought. Comforted by her Japanese etiquette, she consented to being hoisted upon Nagai's back. Sadakichi led the way through brief pools of gentle yellow light that spilled from his wax-paper lantern as they ventured out into the whirl of big snowflakes.

Before a dog barked at them from the street, the city appeared to be at peace and their footsteps were nearly silent on the snow-muffled streets. Nagai screamed back at the stunned party, which froze in place. He became aware of Midori's quick heartbeat and her warm breath on his neck as it slunk away. Now that her life was in jeopardy, Nagai hurriedly went off again, puffing and trying not to startle her. Sadakichi made every effort to stay ahead of the light. Their footsteps reverberated uncannily along the dark wooden corridor as they entered the hospital. As Nagai turned the corner, he noticed that the operation room's lights were on. Steam rose as delicate gray spirals through the shaft of golden light entering from a window and escaped from the room's exhaust pipe. "How lovely everything is," he thought, "steam heating, lights glowing, opeoperating table ready, instruments laid out—everything in readiness to save a precious life".

The procedure was completed seven minutes after they placed her on the operating table. It had been almost time for the appendix to explode. A bewildered Sadakichi, whose emotions had passed through the four seasons in the span of half a night, was given it by a nurse in a bottle of formaldehyde solution.

By now, Tsumo had also shown up, carrying amenities on her back along with sheets and a futon. She also had a bulging furoshiki, which is a common square of colorful cloth used for carrying items by Japanese people. She handed it to Nagai, explaining that it was a small token of appreciation for the good surgeon. When Nagai brought it to the surgeon's room, the surgeon opened it to find a handmade sausage, a ham, and multiple bottles of wine. The surgeon filled his own and Nagai's cups with wine. "To your sweetheart's speedy recovery," he added, lifting his glass. Protesting that Midori was not his sweetheart, Nagai reddened. The young surgeon laughed and said, "Come on, friend." "Are you saying that if she weren't, she would agree to be carried through the streets of Urakami? And how delicately you carried her! It's not something to feel ashamed of. You deserve congratulations for your decision. Let us toast to her.

The Great Pan Is Dead

Nagai was called to the commandant's office and shown to a subordinate's desk a few days after his visit to the brothel. The query, "Who is this Midori, and what's your connection with her?" astonished Nagai as he bowed. "Just an acquaintance, sir, no special connection." "She's only a friend, right? So why are you flushed? The gloves she provided are yours to keep, but this book—A Catholic Catechism—is not. If Special Affairs discovers anything subversive, you will face consequences.

Nagai skimmed the brief note from Midori that was enclosed. But as soon as he opened the glove packaging, he detected the subtle scent of the perfume. He put them to his face and took a breath. The scent that had stuck in his mind ever since he'd kissed her!

The catechism was given to him when he was summoned to the commandant's office three days later. It contains a lot of complex Christian concepts. There is nothing Marxist, according to Special Affairs, but you had best be well-versed in your Soldier's Manual if you have the time to study pointless material about Western gods!

He read the catechism, a simple book with questions and answers, a bit later. The book answered the very questions that had been bothering him for years in clear, although occasionally charming, terms. "What are life's most essential things?" "What gave rise to our birth?" "What is the purpose of pain?" "What's after death?" After switching from atheism to agnosticism, Nagai had given some thought to a number of notable religious personalities in Japan, such as Kobo in the ninth century and Dogen in the thirteenth, who traveled dangerously by sea to China in search of spiritual masters. After returning to Japan, they turned down high-profile jobs and lived austere lifestyles, teaching, writing, and counseling endless streams of people seeking knowledge. Their entire lives had been devoted to finding the answers to the pretty basic issues raised in Midori's catechism. Yes, there were questions and quests, but who knew the answers? Did they exist?

He read the Ten Commandments with shame when he reached them. "I felt unclean all of a sudden. I had lived my entire life abiding by the devil's ten commandments—pride, lust, covetousness, gluttony, anger—if there were a God and a devil. I had done everything the book stated was bad. He garnered his friends' praise on his final day of leave by putting away six bottles of sake and then taking a seat in the busy main street at Senda Machi. All of a sudden, this and a lot of his background felt completely unworthy. What about his future? A premature demise in Manchuria? A devoted woman from Nagasaki who had vowed to pray for him every day was the only bright spot that broke through the darkness. He found solace in her assurance, despite his own inability to believe in Buddha or God.

The narrative from a cordite-acrid Manchuria is continued in Nagai's diary. 2. Two years had passed since the overconfident Japanese army attacked Chinese forces, promising Prime Minister Wakatsuki, who was in shock, that the "Chinese incident" would be resolved quickly. But it had turned into the dreadful "Chinese swamp," and Nagai was constantly laboring on bloody field operating tables.

He describes how difficult it was to explain his decision to amputate to a growing number of amputees. He talks about a soldier who was completely blinded and deaf after being struck by an exploding shell. When the soldier regained consciousness several years later, he believed he was a Chinese prisoner and continually pleaded with them to kill him. His gut churned as Nagai's unit moved forward behind artillery barrages, passing mutilated Chinese dead, many of them infants and elderly.

In the past, his outlook on science and human advancement had been energizing and hopeful. As he worked around the clock, trying to fix his bloodshot eyes on the victims of technological warfare, that vision was now fading like a mirage. He also lost faith in the two-thousand-year sweep of Japanese history and culture. "Japan has a sacred responsibility to occupy the vacuum in Manchuria and stop the advance of inhuman Bolshevism," he had been told by the army in the staging camp near Hiroshima. Japan must likewise usher in the period of Asia Co-prosperity and free Asia from Western colonial rule. He was extremely troubled by the Japanese army's violence.

When Pascal cited the melancholy statement of the Greek author Plutarch, "The great Pan is dead," Nagai lit his hurricane lamp and tiredly opened the Pensées to the point when the pantheon had devolved into "crass superstition or complete atheism." He considered the eight million Shinto gods in the Japanese pantheon.

Pascal continued by insisting that only "if you went down on your knees" could you find the living God. The salty old bell ringer who assisted in the construction of the Urakami Cathedral, along with Midori and her parents, fell on their knees. Prayer, according to Midori's catechism, is as vital to the human spirit as air is to the lungs. Nagai wanted to think that the cosmos and the deaths of young troops in a foreign country, as well as the deaths of his mother and the Chinese mothers, children, and warriors, had some significance. If existence had no ultimate purpose, he might wind up like that blind and deaf soldier, pleading with his "captors" to kill him!

The Machine That Turned on Its Master

That morning, he gave his first lecture to third-year students on x-ray diagnosis. He regarded them solemnly and forewarned of challenging times to come. All of them would be fighting in the war, some on the front lines and others serving as medical officers in areas that would undoubtedly be bombarded. "I feel sure that some of us in this room will be killed or maimed," he said grimly in closing. A vivid vision unexpectedly appeared on his memory screen while he was saying that. He had stolen toys and candy from the Nagasaki Vincentians and brought them to the children's ward at Kanansho Hospital, which is located close to the Yellow River. Some of the kids had no hands or arms, while others had neither. They only looked at him incredulously as he offered them candy. They had lost something more valuable than limbs because of the bombing. A few moments later, his students were staring at him in disbelief as he jolted out of his trance. He cited one of Confucius's favorite sayings, "If you have found the way of truth in the morning, you can meet death peacefully that evening," as much for their support as for his own. He replied, "Now let's get down to x-ray diagnosis," as he brightened.

According to the military government data, Nagai distinguished himself under fire while serving twice at the front. He was ordered very immediately to plan air-raid measures for the Urakami area. The women of the eighteen Neighborhood Associations were among the first organizations he organized. His opening statement, "We may be bombed any time now," shocked the majority of Japanese, who had been lulled into a false sense of security by government propaganda. Learning how to stop bleeding and transport injured people to a first-aid facility are essential. You will need bravery, but more than anything else, you will need love—love that is strong enough to sacrifice your life for your countrymen!

Nagai now focused his efforts on constructing an underground operating room with an x-ray chamber. With a light fastened to his head like a miner, he had worked for days in a makeshift underground theater in China under artillery fire. Some of the university faculty gave him condescending smiles when he told them that the same thing may occur in Nagasaki.

The birth of a daughter helped to ease some of this misery. She was given the name Kayano by Nagai and Midori, which translates to "of the miscanthus reed." The tall, elegant reed known as miscanthus is used to thatch homes, particularly in rural areas. Midori was aware of something about Nagai that is revealed by the choosing of this name. He was deeply enamored with the harmonic fusion of nature and authentic folk craft.

When written in English, Chinese and Japanese names look as sparse as wintered deciduous trees. They seem as banal as "Jones" or "Betty." But they are turned into poetry by the ideographs. The ideographs for "Kayano" evoke images of thatched country houses and waving miscanthus reed. "The well that lasts" is what the ideographs for "Nagai" mean.

Nagai's sobering warnings appeared timid and ridiculous during the early years of Japanese military triumph. But if his students had realized that the American Navy had cracked the Japanese code, the self-assured smiles would have froze. A massive Japanese task force raced into the gray jaws of a steel trap constructed by Admiral Nimitz in June 1942 after the United States had previously analyzed Tokyo's intentions for Midway. The Japanese were unable to reclaim naval momentum for the remainder of the war after losing four large carriers and the finest of its aviation division. However, censorship prevented the Japanese media from covering the Midway disaster. The Japanese march south was stopped when the U.S. Marines landed on Guadalcanal in August 1942.

Japanese supply routes to distant bastions like Lae and Rabaul were being cut off by Allied air dominance by the beginning of 1943. Japan's shipping losses surpassed the amount of tons launched. Nihon had a rough year, but things were going to get much worse. The Japanese mainland had been the target of air raids from far-off Chinese airfields or carrier-based aircraft. The Gilberts, Marshalls, Carolines, and Marianas are small Micronesian island groupings in the central Pacific that were to be seized by the American and British chiefs of staff during a meeting in Cairo in November 1943. The Japanese heroically defended every inch of their territory, but the American steel typhoons overtook Tarawa, the Biak airfield, Saipan, Tinian, and Guam. In July 1944, Saipan was captured, killing 22,000 people and 30,000 Japanese soldiers. Supported by a massive fleet and air force, the U.S. Marines lost more than 14,000 troops.

Nagai inquired about the Catholic teaching on war while getting ready for his baptism. Father Moriyama clarified the custom that Augustine described in the fourth century: one could participate in a "just war." Although he did not believe the Western Allies were models of justice, Nagai had long questioned whether Japan was engaged in a righteous war. With peace of mind, he focused all of his efforts on air-raid drills after realizing that helping the injured, whether they were military or civilians, was in no way immoral. In case the hospital was bombed, he stocked his subterranean theater with medical necessities.

On April 26, 1945, he wrote in his journal of a particularly vicious raid. After it was ended, a truck roaring up to the university hospital was loaded with seriously injured patients. He cleaned human brains off his fingers, assisted in carrying them inside, and sent those who might have had fractures for x-rays. In order to make the corpses appear respectable when family or friends arrived, he then walked down to the morgue to clean them up and suture their wounds. His radiology team detested this task, claiming they had no responsibility for it. They had started attending on a regular basis, though, because he always went down to do it even if no one else did.

The names of graduates murdered while on active duty were presented in news broadcasts with a disturbing regularity. As Nagai detested the undesirable locations in China, he had grown to despise names like Luzon, Leyte, and Iwo Jima. TB rates rose as food shortages throughout the war grew severe. Numerous suspected instances were submitted for x-raying, with Nagai doing a large number of these examinations. As he taught his pupils and performed x-rays on hospital patients, he was also absorbing radiation. Following the deaths of numerous radiologists, including Professor Holzknecht, from cancer brought on by gamma rays leaking from x-ray machines, radiologists came to the conclusion that exposure to more than 0.2 roentgen units per day was hazardous. When questioned by a concerned colleague, Nagai responded, "Yes, I am aware of that, but I am responsible for training our students and I am ultimately responsible for discovering tuberculosis cases," even though he was already well over that limit. People are in danger everywhere in Japan, and if I want to perform my job, I can't escape hazards. He had a false sense of security because he had never been hurt and did not avoid dangerous regions in China. He continued his risky experimentation with gamma rays with more optimism than caution.

However, he started to see warning symptoms on his hands and had severe fatigue, occasionally trembling while climbing stairs. He was an air-raid warden, and night raids meant little sleep. In his journal, he noted that on occasions when he felt completely exhausted, he would shut his office door and sit by himself in front of the Blessed Virgin statue. Calm would gradually return as he recited the Rosary. The nurses saw that he was starting to nod off all around. With a start, he would get up and start working frantically to make up for lost time. Nagai details the result of a colleague's eventual persuasion to have him x-rayed in his book Horobinu Mono Wo.

Standing there with the x-ray frame in his hand, he was aware of how cold it was and how scared and alone he felt. If only he had Midori by his side! How excited he used to be to watch the outcome of a medically fascinating case, and how he had evaluated ten thousand patients in this room. How was he able to be so clinical and aloof? He was now afraid that he might have a terminal illness. He had flung switches and shouted commands with cold impartiality, but many of his patients had been too. His own heart was now encased in ice. His heart felt like a desert, and his lips was parched.

Together, he and the radiologist examined the image, and Nagai let out an involuntary gasp. His spleen was greatly enlarged, and the right side of his stomach was overshadowed by a sinister shadow. His stomach and intestines had been pulled downward, and the upper right portion of his liver was enlarged. His heart has shifted slightly sideways due to upward pressure. The radiologist was speechless. Nagai made an effort to break the tense stillness. "Give your assistant a call so we can try to diagnose him. This has a wealth of useful study material.

Following the lecture, a thorough analysis revealed that his red blood cell level was 40% below normal and his white blood cell count was 1,000 percent higher than usual. Taking the data sheet, he read out loud the medical prognosis: "Patient Nagai has leukemia that is incurable." Two to three years is the life expectancy. Death, cruel and prolonged. He grinned at his sullen companions.

He calmed down as he turned to look at the x-ray equipment that had planted the seeds of doom in his blood before he left. His doctoral thesis had been aided by this equipment. For thousands of his fellow humans, he and this invention had illuminated a path through the darkness. He reasoned that if it had a soul, it would share Nagai's burden and have deep empathy for him. Professor

Suetsugu had brought a sparkling new machine, but it was no longer there. Like Nagai, it was worn there, and the paint chipped off here! Wasn't that the ideal way to die, exhausted from serving your fellow humans? Nagai became aware that his shaking had stopped. Peace and even thankfulness for a full life had returned.

A very soft knock shattered his trance. Come to sympathize, it was the president of the university. Nagai bowed and expressed regret for his negligence. "No, you weren't reckless, Nagai-kun. You are ill because you provided care for those long lines of people in need of assistance when you were the only one available to take their x-rays.

But Midori Will Be beside Me

The most difficult thing he had to do now was to tell Midori the news. Once more in a solemn mood, he strolled slowly home, oblivious to the vibrant hues that the June sun had poured over Nagasaki. Midori had had a difficult life after marrying him. Unlike other professors, he had not established a little surgery at home to augment his meager pay. No, he spent all of his leisure time doing what he enjoyed, which was research. She always waited for him and never grumbled, even though he frequently returned home from university late—sometimes in the wee hours of the morning. "When things are better, we can go to all the restaurants and theaters we like," she said, laughing about the fact that he rarely brought her out. Now, Midori's only option for a future was the difficult path of a young widow because of his assumption and negligence.

With the happy beat of bare feet on tatami, Midori heard the front door slide open and arrived. Her expression brightened. Aren't you home early, then? What a delightful surprise! While humming a tune and discussing having fresh raw tuna and clams for supper, she took off his shoes and assisted him in changing from his Western suit into a kimono. He pondered whether Midori's words were an unconscious attempt to ward them off because he sensed terrible news. What had possessed him to go headfirst into radiology? Like a bear with a painful head, he recalled the times he would be working on an article for a magazine, insisting she not make noise, ordering green tea, and then forgetting to drink it.

When he told her, she appeared to listen emotionlessly. She then lit the candles on their family altar while silently getting up from the table. Her head lowered before the cross her family had protected for 250 years, she knelt there in the austere seiza tradition. Seeing that her shoulders were trembling, he followed her and knelt behind her as well. Until the emotional turmoil had passed, she stayed there in prayer. He was overcome with regret that he had thrown himself carelessly into his own endeavors, assuming Midori would be there. She cocked her head and spoke calmly and gently. "We stated that life and death are wonderful if they are lived for God's glory before we were married and before you traveled to China for the second time. Your work was extremely important, and you gave it your all. He did it for his own glory. Nagai was astounded. He had never been let down by this woman. He was fighting back tears of appreciation, not sorrow for himself. He had the impression that he was surrounded by holiness. At that time, she seemed to represent the persecuted Urakami Christians, who, in spite of 250 years of persecution, continued to believe and hope.

That night, he had entered his house feeling down. He adds that the next day, he was "a new man" when he returned to his x-ray section. I was set free by her total acceptance of the catastrophe and her refusal to listen to any blame-shifting. The physical and emotional exhaustion of the previous months appeared to disappear. She had taken a hefty stone from his chest once more.

After Okinawa fell, there were reports that the United States might land on the island of Kyushu as their next step. As a key port for Kyushu, Nagasaki saw an increase in kenpeitai. After being brought to police headquarters, the Urakami parish priest was questioned regarding the "prayers for peace" being said in the cathedral. "Are you hoping for Japan to lose?" the police chief inquired. "No. Around the world, Christians are praying for peace. It is well acknowledged that war is bad. You certainly do. Yes, the policeman said quickly, "Japan will prevail, and the war will end! Only if you replace your Almighty God with Tenno Heika, the Emperor, will you be able to continue that prayer in your church. In order to avoid being imprisoned like others of his priest friends and having their churches without Mass, the pastor had to carefully consider his response. "But, sir, we have it on the authority of our glorious Emperor Meiji that the Emperor is not Almighty God who made the universe," the elderly priest retorted. "I, in obedience to the grace of heaven," he stated in his Imperial Rescript for Soldiers. We refer to that heaven as Almighty God, and even he obeys it, sir. The priest was advised to return home by the irate authority.

The army predicted that the Americans would soon strike Tokyo Bay and Kyushu and use their feared air force to establish a foothold. However, that would just be the start! The little island of Okinawa was ringed by American ships that bombarded it whenever they wanted, but it took them three months and 12,500 casualties to take it. Japan was over 90% mountainous and could not be encircled by battleships. The Imperial Army and the entire adult population would retreat, as the Chinese did, to the next mountain and then to the next, even if the Americans were to land on coastal plains. Millions of men would have to be lost in years of fighting, or the Americans would have to abandon those "unconditional surrender" terms with the blasphemous threat of the Emperor's execution. To let that happen, every Japanese person would die a thousand deaths. It would be better than such humiliation, even if the race were exterminated.

A group of Catholic lay leaders from Nagasaki were told to report to army headquarters in mid-July 1945. As possible fifth columnists, they were mercilessly reprimanded, threatened, and instructed to report right away to Nagasaki police headquarters in the event that the Americans arrived. One of them, Dr. Nagai, describes how the Christians came to the conclusion that they and their families needed to prepare for the worst—even death. Walking home the long way, Nagai passed the route used by the 26 Christians who were killed in 1597. He specifically begged for assistance in dying as a devout Christian to Saint Paul Miki, whose name he adopted at baptism.

He wrote down his worries about the gradual, agonizing death of patients with his kind of cancer when he returned to the hospital the following day, adding: "But Midori will be beside me." She will place the crucifix on my forehead while she prays. In her embrace, I will breathe my final breath. She'll shut my eyes and transport me to the afterlife. Altruistic Midori! My final moments will be changed by you. Thank you, Midori.

Japan has received a lot of leaflets from the Americans. The Japanese were uncivilized and occasionally comical at initially, but by 1945 they had advanced. Many people read the leaflets against the police's prohibition. A somber poem was included in a recent pamphlet that was dropped on Nagasaki: "In April, Nagasaki was all flowers." There will be flame showers throughout August. August had arrived. Nagai learned of a new bomb that had decimated Hiroshima on the evening of August 6. In the past, he and Midori had attempted to convince their daughters, Kayano, age three, and Makoto, age ten, to accompany Grandma to the country. The parents resisted since the kids were so fussy about it. But what happened on August 6 made the decision. The following day, Grandma and Midori packed their knapsacks with supplies and walked northeast with the kids to a rural home in Koba that looked out over a serene mountain valley. They were greeted by a singing mountain stream and a cacophonous ensemble of cicadas.

Early the following morning, the ninth, Midori went back home. She and Nagai went to their bunker when an air-raid warning went off. She placed his arm over her shoulder and her arm around his waist because he was physically in poor condition, with his legs shaky and his spleen bloated. He burst out laughing, and she did too. He describes how they sat in their shelter like picnicking lovers. On August 15, a significant day for Nagasaki Christians and the day Francis Xavier arrived in Japan, they talked about the upcoming feast of the Assumption and forgot about the war. When Midori offered to prepare the customary bean-jam cakes, he chuckled at how many their boy Makoto had consumed on the previous Assumption Day. In anticipation of the feast day, Nagai inquired about the hours for confession. Midori informed him that she would be leaving early tomorrow. He stated that a better time for him would be tomorrow afternoon.

After receiving the all-clear, they made their way back to the residence. The fact that Midori was in a state of "positive gaiety" astounded and pleased him. While they ate breakfast together, she laughed about their young imps in the mountains and how difficult it was for Grandma to deal with them. He declined, saying he felt alright today, when Midori offered to walk him to the university. She assisted him in putting on his white shoes at the genkan, or front porch. He goes on to say that she was beaming as she knelt on the tatami and bowed low to him while saying the customary and sweet goodbye, "Itte irasshai mase." Trying not to look wobbly, he bowed and replied heartily, "Itte mairimasu," before leaving with his stick, thinking, "This is wonderful; she's in such fine spirits despite everything."

He recalled leaving his lunch, an o-bento, in the kitchen, just a short distance down the street. He got a great shock when he went back to the genkan. Midori lay on the tatami, trembling like a kid as she sobbed!

That evening, August 8, he was on air-raid duty and declined a request to be removed from the list. "Observe how outstanding the student wardens have been throughout the air raids; some of them have even lost their lives as a result. No, they have not requested any compromises, and I will not either. The radiology dean aspired to set a personal example for his students and young employees.

An air-raid warning went off on August 9th, but it was only a single plane, and the all-clear went off at 10 a.m. Someone said, "Time wasted on a plane not interested in Nagasaki." He was mistaken; it was highly interested and radioed accurate information back to a B-29 called Bock's Car, which was racing from Tinian north to Japan.

After the 10 a.m. alarm, Midori left the shelter with two relatives, Grandma Urata and Tatsue, and they sat on her balcony and chatted. Gran responded, "Your kids must be lonely." Midori was preparing to make bean-jam cakes by laying out a bag of beans to dry in the sun. She said, "Yes, Gran." Anyway, Kayano. Makoto, the urchin, will be swimming in the river with a frog-like level of happiness. He will eventually develop webbed fingers. Gran's face became hazy as she said, "And the good doctor, how is he, Midori?" after laughing. "I fear he is evil. He is so ill that no one could work as hard as he does without getting worse. I haven't seen him since breakfast yesterday since he was on air-raid duty last night. I'm quite concerned about him. Please continue to pray for him. Gran gave a solemn nod. When she was younger, she would go with the younger woman on Midori's occasional four-mile trek to the Lourdes Grotto, which is located behind the monastery on the city's eastern borders. When Father Maximilian Kolbe arrived in Nagasaki in May 1931, he constructed that grotto.

At that moment, a second young cousin walked into the yard with ease. "O-hayo gozaimasu." "Good morning," she sang fairly. "Who wants to grind wheat by walking to Topposui Mill? Will someone not accompany me on a stunning country road that is simply awaiting visitors beneath a blue sky? Tatsue responded, "Yes, I'd go," grinning at her younger relative's enthusiasm. Kikue turned to Midori and clasped her hands, saying, "Now, distinguished head of all the Women's Associations of Urakami. "It is important that children develop freedom and grace of bodily movement, as well as a sense of beauty," you stated during our most recent meeting, and I can quote you. You must therefore accompany us as we gracefully and freely swing our arms and legs to Topposui and take in the endless splendor. Midori said she had wheat to grind but would visit the mill on her way to see her kids later in the day because she liked the jokes. Since her husband wasn't home the previous evening, she had to prepare his lunch and deliver it to him at the hospital. Tatsue Urata describes their parting in moving detail in the novel We of Nagasaki. "We divided into two groups in this way: the ones that would be safe and the ones that would be killed."

When the Sun Turned Black

Major "Chuck" Sweeney had an extraordinarily perilous takeoff before daybreak, loaded as he did with the 4.5-ton A-bomb, "Fat Man". They had now surpassed Kokura, their main objective. After three trips over the bleakly overcast metropolis, he discovered something startling: the auxiliary gasoline hose was obstructed. They would never return home unless they dropped the bomb quickly. In order to reach the secondary target, "Nagasaki, urban area," he steered his aircraft southwest.

Just before eleven in the morning, his B-29 was above Shimabara. When a radio announcer heard this, he excitedly issued a warning, and the inhabitants of Nagasaki rushed to their shelters.

Following the all-clear, confessions were being heard once more within the Urakami Cathedral by Fathers Nishida and Tamaya. Fat Man exploded just a third of a mile from the cathedral, which was instantly destroyed. Nobody would know how many people died inside.

Chimoto-san was cultivating his rice paddies on Mount Kawabira, less than two miles from the church. A B-29 appeared out of the clouds when he looked up after hearing a disturbance. He hurled himself to the ground as it disgorged a massive black bomb. He held off for a minute. Then there was a terrible, piercing light, and then a strange silence. He gasped when he saw the enormous pillar of smoke rising, grotesquely growing. He became acutely aware that a cyclone was speeding in his direction. Before his shocked eyes, houses, buildings, and trees were being felled as though by some massive, unseen bulldozer. Then there was a thunderous roar, and he was flung sixteen feet behind him into the stone wall like a matchbox. The pines, chestnuts, and camphor laurels that had been ripped from the ground or snapped off at the trunks left him speechless. There was no grass left!

Sadako Moriyama, Midori's nineteen-year-old cousin, had just discovered her two younger brothers in the Yamazato schoolyard, chasing dragonflies. Their mother wanted them, she informed them. She hurried with them to the school shelter as soon as she heard the plane. She passed out as they were lifted up and flung to the far wall as they entered. She heard the two kids whimpering at her feet as she woke up and pondered why it was so dark.

She stepped outside. It was dim, as though it were just beginning to dawn. When she saw four naked toddlers next to the sandbox, she let out a loud cry! Her eyes unconsciously drank in the gruesome details as she stood there enthralled. Their hands resembled gloves turned inside out, with the skin peeled away at the wrists and hanging from their fingernails.

She rushed back into the shelter, feeling as like she was losing her mind, and unintentionally brushed past the two victims who were still writhing and groaning close to the door. Their bodies had the texture of rotten potatoes. They resumed their dreadful animal croaking. They were saying something, she realized. Mizu, mizu. Water, water. For years, that cry would reverberate in the nightmares of those who survived Nagasaki.

Ten-year-old Michiko Ogino was spending the summer vacation at home. She was frightened by a massive lightning flash shortly after eleven in the morning, which was followed by a terrible roar. In a matter of seconds, she was among the thousands of people trapped beneath their homes' walls or roofs. Houses were flattened when the bomb exploded, sending air rushing from the epicenter at more than a mile per second. An equally strong wind poured back into the void left at the epicenter almost instantly.

When Michiko screamed, a stranger arrived and removed her from the hopeless pin. She was shocked to see ominous clouds outside that writhed and twisted, blotting out the sun. How could this have been caused by fresh lightning? And then she heard a small voice going frantic. Her two-year-old sister was stranded beneath a crossbeam. When she turned to seek assistance, she noticed a nude woman running at them; her hair was frizzed out and reddish brown, and her body was oily and purple like an eggplant. Oh no! Mother was there! Michiko was unable to speak and could only gesture to her sister beneath the beam. The mother dove amid the debris, placed her shoulder beneath the beam, and heaved after glancing anxiously at the already-started fires. With the two-year-old free, the mother fell to the ground, holding her to her breast. The shoulder she had placed beneath the beam was covered in raw, gushing meat with no skin remaining. Michiko's father also showed there, severely burned. His wife moaned and struggled to get up, as he stared in stupid helplessness. Then she lost all of her power and fell to the ground, lifeless.

Sakue Kawasaki sat in the Aburagi air-raid shelter, stunned by the news that Nagasaki was now on fire. Outside, he could see naked, pumpkin-swollen humans stumbling around. After that, there was a cacophony of croaking voices pleading for mizu, mizu, but where could he find water? One of the victims crept over to a puddle of filthy water outside the shelter's entrance, sank his mouth into it, and drank with delectable moans. He fell and stopped moving when he attempted to crawl to the shelter. The others curled up still, drinking from the puddle one by one. What kind of dreadful need could make mankind behave like insane lemmings?

Although there were significant variances, the plutonium-239 bomb detonated in Nagasaki with the same amount of force as 22,000 tons of conventional explosives. The deadly radiation from the A-bomb was temporarily set aside in favor of its extreme heat, which at the site of explosion reached several million degrees Celsius. More than half a mile from the epicenter, the air surrounding the massive bomb became bright, emitted infrared and ultraviolet rays, and blistered roof tiles as its entire mass was ionized and a fireball was formed. Up to 2.5 miles distant, exposed human skin was burnt. On the surface facing the explosion, buildings, trees, and electric light poles within two miles were scorched. The wind that raced out from the epicenter had a speed of over one mile per second, which is sixty times faster than a big cyclone. A cyclone surged back in, carrying with it acres of dust, dirt, debris, and smoke, darkening the writhing mushroom cloud. This created a vacuum at the epicenter.

Five kilometers south of the epicenter, on a mountainside outside Oyama, young Kato-san was strolling with his cow. Startled by the brightness, he stood motionless and watched as a massive white cloud rose up like a hideous creature gaining weight via some strange power. Despite having a white exterior, the cloud was fueled by a repulsive red energy. Then there were flashes of purple, yellow, and red that alternated. A black stain developed on the stem of the cloud as it gradually took on the shape of a mushroom. As the cloud rose to a considerable height, it exploded and fell apart like a foul-smelling grub that had eaten too much.

The light shone on the surrounding mountains, but the region beneath the cloud was gloomy. Then came Kato's second shock, a windstorm so powerful that Kato thought it was another bomb going off nearby.

And the Rain Turned to Poison

At 10 a.m. on August 9, Dr. Nagai had emerged from the hospital air-raid bunker when the all-clear was sounded. He put on his heavy warden's equipment and steel helmet, relieved to see sunlight and breathe clean air once more. He stopped for a time, letting his tired eyes take in the dark purple of the tiled roofs below him and the blood crimson of the oleander and canna in the hospital garden. His gaze swept over Nagasaki Bay, which was gorgeously framed by the sheer white clouds floating across the bluest of skies and the summer green of Mount Inasa. Kuni yaburete sanga ari, a quote from the ancient Chinese poet Toho, sprang to mind as he thought, "So peaceful, and what a contrast to our war-torn world." Even if the country is destroyed, the rivers and mountains will still exist. But he needed to get to work! He rushed back to the hospital, regrettably averting his gaze from the ever-new beauty of nature. He was sitting in his office getting ready to give a lecture an hour later.

Shortly after eleven in the morning, a burst of dazzling light appeared. There's a bomb near the university entrance, I thought. I wanted to jump to the ground straight away, but before I could do so, windowpane glass burst through with a startling sound. I felt like I was thrown ten feet by a gigantic hand. Glass fragments scattered like leaves in a tornado. With my eyes wide, I caught a view of the exterior, where clothes, beams, and planks were dancing strangely in the air. I thought the end was near since everything in my own room had joined in. Warm blood ran down my neck and cheek from the glass cut on my right side. Everything in the office was being smashed by the irrational big invisible fist. As I listened to odd sounds like mountains shaking back and forth, various objects dropped on top of me. Then it was completely dark, as though the hospital, which was made of reinforced concrete, had suddenly sped into a tunnel like an express train. I had not yet experienced any pain, but as I smelled acrid smoke and heard crackling flames, panic took hold of my heart. I focused all of my attention on the Lord, our Judge, and begged for forgiveness since I was aware of my transgressions, particularly the three I had planned to confess that afternoon.

In the x-ray room next door was Nurse Hashimoto. She was protected by an anchored bookcase and held firmly against the wall as she observed the strange movement of the room's movable items. She stumbled and proceeded to peek out a window when everything stopped. There was no more sea of dwellings below! Across the bay from Mount Inasa, the vivid summer green had vanished, leaving only a crimson surface. There were no trees or grass anywhere she looked. The entire planet appeared to be nude. She gasped as she saw the ruined grounds with nude bodies entangled in rubble near the front entrance. No sound was heard. Was the world dead? She put her palms over her eyes to keep the fear out. "Hell is visible to me! "Hell!" she angrily exclaimed. When she opened her eyes once again, Dante's Inferno was still playing. The seventeen-year-old nurse was certain that her time was running out as darkness descended as though to cover all hope. She started to whimper like a kid and quiver convulsively.

Then she heard the cries, "Help, help!" which reminded her that she was an adult and came as a double slap in the face. Dean Nagai was there! She attempted to enter his chamber, but she realized she would want assistance because the path was severely obstructed by broken equipment. She ran against something soft as she felt her way down the dim hallway. Her hand got sticky and damp as she knelt down. Searching for a pulse, she located an arm. None existed. She joined her hands in a quick prayer and continued. The darkness was abruptly broken by the blaze of scarlet flames. She had to hurry, she was informed by sharp crackling sounds.

Half a mile from the epicenter, this reinforced concrete hospital was not destroyed by the atom bomb, but 80 percent of the patients and staff died. With the best protection, the x-ray section was located at the southeast end. Five of the x-ray employees were located by Nurse Hashimoto, who then escorted them back. They liberated Dr. Nagai by forming a human chain and breaking through a window. He was well-prepared by his wartime experiences in China, and his composure soothed them.

Nagai's students were struggling elsewhere on campus. All of his first-year students were pinned like butterflies on a specimen board after the hefty roof above them collapsed. Despite his best efforts, head student Fujimoto was unable to raise the masonry off his shoulders and head. A number of kids started an odd discussion. The roaring flames crept in on them, and it was over.

His team came back. With all of the valves damaged, the electric wires in ruins, and the transformer buried beneath a pile of debris, the x-ray equipment was a write-off. Nagai stared around at the faces, unable to think or even speak. We can't panic, he told himself. But we will be roasted to death if we do nothing. However, not a single useful concept emerged. He suddenly burst out laughing nervously. The incongruity caused everyone to laugh. Although it was unexpected, it eased the strain.

The pandemonium outside the hospital seemed unsettling. Heads or limbs were gone, and bodies hung upside down on fences and stone walls. Two youngsters dragged their father up the hill while a wild-eyed mother rushed past with a child who had been decapitated. Quite insanely, a man was singing and dancing on the roof of a burning building across the street. A calm elderly couple strolled up the hill, hand in hand, away from the sea of flames that roared below. However, Nagai and his team were unable to do anything but watch as the hospital was engulfed in flames.

When more x-ray personnel arrived, one of them inquired, "Should we try to haul the equipment out?" "No," Nagai said, "forget it." Patients will be burned alive in certain wards. First, go there. Go! He hurried to the subterranean emergency room himself. Everything was inundated with water due to burst pipes. In a frantic mess, stretchers, medications, and instruments were broken and mixed together. "I felt like a mosquito with its legs severed." He reflected, "All we have left is our knowledge, our love, and our bare hands," realizing that they had reached their lowest point. Upon ascending the steps, he gazed uncomfortably at the peculiar mushroom cloud that loomed menacingly over Nagasaki. In the meantime, his nurses were hauling patients out of the smoke-filled wards while tying damp hand towels around their faces.

The afternoon had arrived. Dr. Okura went up to Nagai, young. In the ward, there is still a patient with arthritis. Unless I obtain a stretcher, he won't go. No stretchers are present. Nagai gazed at the flames, which were thirty-three feet high and were being fueled by the wind coming in from the west. They were situated on Mount Konpira's slopes on the east side of the hospital. It seems suicide for Okura to go back to the ward. "Go away from the patient. "I accept responsibility," Nagai declared. Even though it was plain sense, Nagai and the majority of the survivors would later suffer from regret as they thought about the person they might have rescued, "had we not left them to perish while we saved our own skin."

Blood first gushed forth "like red ink from a water pistol" after flying glass damaged Nagai's temporal artery. The wound had been tightly bandaged and packed by his personnel. The bleeding continued despite this, and he was now a man with a red turban. The west wind pushed the fires nearer to the ground where the rescued patients were lying.

He looked around when the heaving in his chest subsided and noticed that everything that had been organized was starting to fall apart. From the city below, more people were arriving in hopes of finding comfort at the large hospital complex. The staff was barely able to touch their own patients, and their expressions were starting to exhibit signs of worry. This couldn't be further from the truth. "All of a sudden, it seemed completely beyond us, and we started to lose our nerve," recalled Matron [Head Nurse] Hisamatsu, who is still a resident of Nagasaki. Nagai yelled, "Find a Hi no Maru," the Japanese flag, at that moment. He gave the order to young Dr. Okura, who at that moment could not imagine anything so trivial as a flag! "It's impossible to find one," he stated after going through the motions of searching for one in the few areas that weren't on fire. As the white sheet flew in his direction, Nagai glanced at it. In order to create a rough red circle, he grabbed it, tore it into a square, removed the blood-soaked bandage from his head, and squeezed and dabbed blood into the center. The Japanese flag appeared after Matron Hisamatsu and a few others added blood from their own wounds.

Nagai had seen firsthand during the Chinese war how a daring deed or a potent symbol may occasionally reverse the centrifugal forces of shock and panic. The national flag, Hi no Maru, was the most potent emblem for Japanese people in 1945. The militarists had ensured that it flew above all military headquarters, public buildings, and significant events over the previous fifteen years. Nagai gave Okura instructions to drive the improvised flag into a grassy area a short distance above them and tie it to a sturdy bamboo pole that was laying there. Forty-two years later, Matron Hisamatsu remembers it clearly: "All of a sudden, we had a 'headquarters' to rally around, a center that put order back into the picture." "It was such a simple act, and yet the psychological effect was profound," concurs Dr. Okura, who is now a priest and (importantly) an authority on Saint John of the Cross.

Mother Nature had always been a source of solace and support for Nagai throughout difficult times. He was shocked to learn that even her had been unhinged by the blast. Flat drops of black rain started to fall, leaving behind stains of evil and darkness. The air had also become sour. As the fires spread out, they were consuming so much oxygen that they were emitting so much carbon dioxide that Nagai and his colleagues were gasping for air.

Five hours after the devastating explosion, it was now 4 PM, and the fires were still raging ferociously. Patients groaned—some in agony, some in fear—but the only thing the medical team could do was remove glass splinters or wood fragments and cement, frequently using rudimentary tools, apply a small amount of iodine, and bandage the larger wounds. They tried to quench the shouts of "Mizu, mizu!" by fetching large amounts of water from wells and a nearby mountain stream.

When Nagai discovered the university president lying ill in a field, his white coat stained with black rain, tears welled up in his eyes. After giving the slack-jawed president a brief update, he went back to work. Nagai removed his coat and covered Umezusan, the x-ray technician, who was drenched through and fell on the ground.

Nagai had felt a strong want to run down and look for Midori ever before he noticed the entire Urakami area was on fire at around midday. However, he was aware that would be gravely incorrect. As more people staggered up from the suburbs below, the situation only got worse for him, who was one of the few authority officials standing. He continued to sneak peeks, praying and expecting to spot her among the migrants. However, Midori was nowhere to be seen by 4 PM, and a horrible despair descended upon him. He paused his work and peered down at the Urakami suburb. Now, just the black concrete shells of a few public buildings and the ragged remains of the cathedral walls remained. His residence was surrounded by a smoldering, flat ash desert. Then the certainty of her death hit him like a blow to the body. He had already pushed his body and mind over their limits. A coworker overheard him murmuring, "She would have arrived by now," as his legs suddenly became floppy and buckled and he fell to the ground. She is indeed deceased. "Miori!" After purposefully crushing a fistful of earth with one hand, he passed out, primarily from blood loss.

When he came to, Professor Fuse was yelling nervously, "Thread." Forceps. Gauze, gauze. The end of the artery has slipped behind the bone, so apply pressure! Nagai lost consciousness once more, but the bleeding had ceased. When he opened his eyes again, he saw a small portion of the moon over the desolate Mount Inasa. While the soldiers constructed lean-to shelters for the injured and patients, the nurses gathered pumpkins from the nearby fields and boiled them in air-raid helmets. Nagai's gaze landed on two small, young nurses who were hard at work.

Dr. Nagai stood up and joined the small group of doctors, nurses, x-ray techs, and his coworkers. "We felt that we were bound together by some incomprehensible fate as we looked at one another," he writes. We simply sat there in silence while clutching each other's hands tightly.

The Last Black Hole in the Universe?

Even though the sun had set, physicians and nurses were still combing the nearby fields for survivors while massive fires burned below. Doctors and nurses continued searching in the dark for the injured, many of whom did not make it all the way up from the city to the hospital hill. As they stumbled along carrying the injured, the rescuers frequently slipped and cut themselves on broken glass or fell headlong into culverts, not realizing that a bridge had vanished. Many feet had been injured by boards with exposed nails that had been thrown in all directions. The fires below were extinguishing by midnight when Matron Hisamatsu spoke the frantic words, "Doctor, the cathedral is going up in flames." Constructed to stand alone on a hill, it had been destroyed in the first explosion but had escaped burning along with the other wooden Urakami. But at last, flying sparks lit its shattered timbers, and suddenly, like dancers in a horrific ballet, immense red flames erupted. He stared in awe until the cathedral's death rattle was announced by a loud crash of bricks and timbers. Nagai would never be able to forget that moment.

He thought that the classic Greek tragedy of World War II appeared to be nearing its apocalyptic conclusion. A lumbering B-29 had brought a deus ex machina to the center stage. The scientific era of enlightenment produced this strange bomb of a deus, this new god! The Book of Revelation's horror and grandeur were all that Nagai, the believer, could think about. The shattered cathedral rested like the slain Lamb. The unusual cloud that appeared to be absorbing energy from the burning below caught Nagai's attention. What was the new bomb that exploded like black magic, and what was it?

The doctor and his team woke up from a restless sleep with the dawn, stunned by the scene of nuclear ash all around them and below. Nothing green, nothing living. Nothing, no cicadas, no summer sounds. In the hopes of discovering some tools and medication, they dragged themselves back to the destroyed hospital. There were burnt bodies and skeletons everywhere. They discovered professors, students, doctors, nurses, technicians, and patients reduced to charred lumps in the rooms where their pals had been at 11:02 a.m. the previous day. Some laid with their hands up above their heads, while others were crowded in a row. Nagai bowed his head and said a quick prayer.

With a leaflet dropped by a U.S. plane telling the populace to evacuate the city before it was too late, Matron Hisamatsu ran up to Nagai.

Nagai glanced over the message and then yelled uncontrollably: "The atom bomb! It had to be that, indeed! It became evident when the astounding devastation in Nagasaki was combined with all the information long conjectured about atomic fission. "At that moment, conflicting emotions churned within me: a triumph for physics and a tragedy for Japan; the victory of science and the defeat of my country." At his feet was a bamboo spear, one of the weapons women had been practicing with since the General Mobilization Ordinance was established on August 14, 1944, mandating that all females aged thirteen to sixty engage in regular practice with bamboo spears. The wives, kids, and grandmothers of ancient samurai who fought on the battlefield with such weapons when their castle was in danger were to confront the invading Americans. Atom bombs versus bamboo spears! "Will we Japanese be now forced to stand on our shores and be annihilated without a protest?" Nagai thought as he kicked the frail weapon in desperation and rage.

He brought the pamphlet to Professor Seiki, a renowned scientist who was lying on the exposed ground in a temporary air-raid bunker. After reading it, Seiki moaned and spent a considerable amount of time staring at the empty sky. He then started a conversation with the nearby scientists in his trademarkly smart manner. As Nagai puts it, "as strange as it seems, we became completely absorbed, oblivious of everything else." The army had halted the expensive uranium-235 research that Japanese scientists had been doing. In the West, who had made the breakthrough? The Joliot-Curies, Madame Meitner, Hahn, Dohr, Fermi, Chadwick, and Einstein were among the prewar front-runners they suggested. Seiki then raised the irrelevant topic of the radiation that results from atom splitting.

A feeling of astonishment had been bestowed onto Nagai. When he glanced up at old friends like the North Star or the Great Bear constellation, "they evoked a sense of intimate kinship in my heart," he could be carried away on a clear night. He now squatted on the barren earth next to the distinguished Professor Seiki and talked animatedly about radiation as though it were unimportant to him personally, aware only of the chance to "participate in a precious scientific experience." He and his colleagues would now use this hillside as an experimental table to learn more about the effects of the hotly contested atomic fission on people, insects, and plants. They were enraged and distraught about what had happened to their people yesterday. They felt "a new dynamism and motivation in our quest for truth" today. Something was already sprouting on this wrecked nuclear wilderness: the robust seedlings of fresh scientific information.

To cater to the victims, Nagai forced himself to leave the intriguing conversation. In the daytime, it was now easier to see the destructive force of the wind produced by the atomic fission. For example, he discovered heads severed at the neck, seemingly by a gigantic blade. It was also painfully clear that fission-released infrared rays were extremely hot. The prevalence of gamma-ray illness sharply rose. Some claimed to have had seasickness or a severe hangover, while others claimed to have felt as though they had breathed town gas. Those who believed they had escaped unharmed started to slouch in the closest shade, too ill to move. Nagai was now experiencing his own illness. Although this twofold dose of gamma radiation was extremely upsetting, it gave him the opportunity to investigate the effects of A-bomb radiation both scientifically and firsthand.

On August 10, Nagai and his friends were frightened when American aircraft continued to cruise overhead. They were unable to determine whether these aircraft were carrying further A-bombs. They would frantically dive for cover when they heard a jet, moving as methodically as they could among the fallen to see if any were alive.

As they stared at the horrifying images of people who had been skinned alive or reduced to large chunks of charcoal, a certain neurosis started to take hold. Every enemy plane sound was like an electric shock to bare nerves. As limbs became more leaden and their mission appeared more hopeless, a sort of psychological vertigo took control. Sick with radiation nausea and despair, they fell to the clay floor of their bunker when darkness fell on the tenth. Was that a shelter, really? Or was that a universe's final black hole exploding in on itself? There were a lot of groaning, restless bodies on the shelter floor. Some of them eventually turned into corpses, but nobody had the strength to take them out. The name of Oyanagi-san, a nurse who had passed away the day before, was yelled by someone who gripped Nagai's shoulders in a nightmare at around midnight.

High Noon, and a Nation Wept

Grandma Moriyama made the tragic trip to Urakami the day after the A-bomb dropped, returning with a few pieces of Midori's bones in a tiny metal container. She warned Makoto not to investigate, but his suspicions were sparked by the respectful manner in which she handled it and her constant tears, so after she was gone for a while, he slipped over, shaky, and opened it. He had a gut feeling that the bones belonged to his mother. The sliding door clattered back unexpectedly a few days later while the youngster and his grandma sat at a thrifty table, glum and silent. They were initially unable to identify the gaunt, unshaven man who was standing there with his clothes ripped and dirty, a blood-stained bandage covering the majority of his head. Little Kayano cried and fled in fear behind Gran as he tried to pick her up. The homecoming was depressing.

Nagai soon learned that many A-bomb victims had been transported, hauled, or had staggered to this chilly mountain region with its crystal-clear stream and mineral spring, which was known to aid in the healing of burns. The poor casualties had been welcomed with great generosity by the nearby farmers. Over a hundred people were being housed by one neighbor, Takami-san. Others, with glass, concrete, and wooden splinters embedded in them, could be helped, but many were horribly bloated and dying. Despite their severe lack of supplies and equipment, his small group of survivors from the x-ray department kept their meeting with him the following day and made the decision to start a mobile medical unit in Koba. They leave early every morning to treat patients all across the valley, extracting glass splinters and other debris and tending to wounds that are festering. They found that the mineral spring water cured burns, but they were unable to help the numerous radiation illness victims. They would get home late every night, fatigued, and there were always too many patients.

It wasn't all laborious. The nostalgic sense of "inhaling the fragrance of summer grasses and washing away our grime and weariness in swift mountain streams" is described by city inhabitant Nagai. He noticed reminders of his new motto everywhere he went on the pristine country roads. The mountains that remained motionless in the face of strong winds, fog, and rain were the ever-faithful God's fingerprints. He would look up in awe at the dark fields covered with astral grain on clear mountain evenings. He thought about the constellation Virgo. According to the ancient Greek myth, Virgo abandoned earth in search of a chaste location in the heavens because she was so troubled by the wicked ways of mankind. Virgo was similar to Hamazaki and every other nurse in his department who perished as a result of military men's immoral behavior. How unfortunate that these young ladies would never experience a husband's touch or a child's smile!

The Imperial Army formations positioned in Japan proper and on the Asian mainland were essentially neutralized by the crippling of Japan's air force and navy well before August. Sensible Japanese authorities realized the war was lost and were prepared for peace when American aircraft destroyed ports and factories virtually at will. In an attempt to recruit Russia as a peace mediator with the West, Prime Minister Suzuki sent Foreign Minister Togo to Moscow; however, Russia was holding off until Japan was sufficiently vulnerable to be invaded without consequence. The White House was being persuaded by a powerful group of Americans that "unconditional surrender" had little chance of being accepted by Japan since it did not acknowledge the Emperor's holy position. Joseph Grew, who served as the American ambassador in Tokyo prior to the start of the Pacific War, was in charge of this organization. Grew "had a rare understanding and affection for Japan and all things Japanese," according to historian

Toland. Grew maintained that the Emperor was not a war criminal and had attempted to stop the war, citing his ten years of experience in Japan and his firsthand knowledge of the origins of the conflict. He went on to say that the majority of Japanese would not collaborate with an occupation that approved of such a sacrificial act and would oppose a surrender that would result in the Emperor being tried as a war criminal. Some Far Eastern specialists at the State Department, including Professor Blakeslee, Dooman, and Ballantine, as well as Assistant Secretary of War McCloy, firmly backed Grew. On July 27, 1945, the Allies broadcast the Potsdam Proclamation for unconditional surrender after their case was dismissed. 1 Prime Minister Suzuki, who was 78 years old, longed for peace—but peace that would safeguard the Emperor. He responded to the Allies on July 28 by using the phrase mokusatsu, which translates to "rejection." Accepting that decision, the Japanese prepared for the difficult battles that would follow the American landing. The A-bombing of Hiroshima on August 6 was not reported by the Japanese media.

In light of the recent events in Hiroshima, the Supreme Council of War convened at 11 a.m. on August 9 to deliberate on the Potsdam demand. The Emperor was present at the gathering as a spectator, as was customary. Prime Minister Suzuki, Foreign Minister Togo, and Navy Minister Admiral Yonai were three of the six council members who supported unconditional surrender. Army Chief General Umezu, Navy Chief Admiral Toyoda, and War Minister General Anami all vehemently opposed it. The meeting was called off because of the hopeless impasse.

The Emperor was devastated when he learned of the second A-bomb dropped on Nagasaki a few hours later. Would he be held accountable if his people were exterminated if he persisted in his passive "reign"? He made the lonesome decision to call a meeting of the Supreme War

Council, all cabinet ministers, and high imperial officials in his air raid bunker at midnight. He quickly declared that Japan would agree to Potsdam's requirements after they had assembled in his bunker and made fun of him. The audience was as taken aback as though a stone crane that was two thousand years old had just spoken! The majority of his audience cried, and some of them wailed aloud. Breaking all previous records, the Emperor said that he would personally broadcast this to the country.

Nagai and the rest of Japan assumed they would hear an order to repel the Americans, just as their forebears had done when they repelled the Mongol army in the thirteenth century, when they were instructed to stand by their radio sets at noon on August 15. When the high-pitched voice of the Chrysanthemum Throne told them they "must bear the unbearable and suffer the insufferable," they were taken aback. That implied complete and utter surrender. People in Japan started crying, and many of them knelt down with their foreheads on the ground, facing the Emperor in sorrow. Our Japan, represented by Mount Fuji emerging through the clouds, the first mountain to be kissed by the sun's rays when it rises in the East, was dead, according to Nagai, who describes the shock of "unconditional surrender" to him. An abyss was being plunged into by our race!

They ate a small breakfast the following morning and sat in near complete quiet, not even trying to wash the dishes. A man knocked on the door, requesting a doctor to visit a buddy who was ill. "One sick man makes no difference when the whole nation is doomed," Nagai passionately yelled at him. They watched the shocked man traverse the fields and return, forlorn. Nagai abruptly changed his mind and sent Little Bean running after him. The weary group resumed its medical rounds after following Nagai. Their endurance had significantly decreased, though, and they were now experiencing the side effects of radiation as well: fatigue, hair loss, bleeding gums, fever, and an irregular white blood cell count. Nagai began exhibiting serious signs of A-bomb illness on September 8, 1945. For a week, his temperature remained at 104 degrees. His face was the size of a soccer ball, and his entire body was bloated. Bleeding resumed as the flesh surrounding his temporal incision decayed, producing a gaping wound. Day and night, Nurse Morita and Dr. Tomita alternated applying pressure to the temporal artery. If not, he would die from bleeding within three hours. He had already lost a significant amount of blood, and his heartbeat and pulse were clearly beginning to fail. He was injected by someone. According to the discomfort, Nagai thought, "Ah, nikethamide." Nagai claimed he wanted to make a broad confession when Father Tagawa arrived.

The clear autumn sky outside the window served as the inspiration for Nagai's farewell song. With feeble brushstrokes, he said goodbye to a world that had brought him great joy:

Kie ni Keri. Hikari tsu tsu Aki-zora takaku.

A bright and lofty fall sky... I go.

He fell unconscious shortly after finishing his poetry. His breathing had gotten worse when his eyes opened again, and he estimated that he was a few hours away from passing away. "Cheyne-Stokes breathing," he whispered, looking at Dr. Tomita pressing on his temporal artery. "Yes," said Tomita. Now, Nagai described the sensation in his chest as "like an empty car lurching around inside." In the hopes that a university colleague could have guidance or medication to help Nagai survive, Dr. Fuse had traveled to Nagasaki.

He was able to locate Doctors Cho, Kageura, and Koyano, three medical university professors. Each responded in the same way when Fuse explained the symptoms: Nagai is dying, and there is nothing that can be done about it.

Now that he was unable to move his head or open his eyes, Nagai, who had been slipping in and out of a coma, thought, "Convulsions will soon begin." He could hear his son's voice and the prayers. He wanted to live because of that. A woman's voice spoke in a comforting tone. That's Gran, I see. She whispered softly, "This is water from our Lady's grotto at Hongochi Monastery." Her words conjured up a vivid picture of the Lourdes Grotto and the reassuring face of Mary the Mother of God. "How, I don't know, but I heard—I heard it alone, and I heard it clearly—a voice telling me to ask Father Maximilian Kolbe to pray for me," Nagai went on. I followed instructions and prayed to Father Kolbe. "Lord, I leave myself in your divine hands," I said, turning to face Christ.

After applying pressure to the ruptured artery, Nurse Morita abruptly turned to Dr. Tomita and declared, "The bleeding has stopped!" Without medical assistance, the big wound that had defied medicine had healed. In one of his subsequent novels, Nagai described the event in great detail. He stated that he and the accompanying physicians thought his recovery was amazing, but that it is always possible to be wrong when it comes to miraculous cures. He swiftly went on to say that miraculous healings are not indicative of holiness, pointing out that at sites like Lourdes, incidents that panels of medical experts have deemed medically inexplicable involve people who have little or no faith.

Nagai attributed his recuperation to Father Kolbe. In 1930, Kolbe, a Polish Franciscan, arrived in Japan. He established a monastery in

Nagasaki and constructed a Lourdes grotto behind it, which is now a popular destination for pilgrims from all across the country. The Marian weekly he founded continues to be the most read publication in Catholic Japan. He was well known to Nagai, who had x-rayed him for tuberculosis. Kolbe was called back to Poland in 1936 to serve as the prior of a sizable monastery. The monastery started publishing Catholic periodicals under his leadership, and each week they sold millions of copies. The Nazi occupiers quickly became aware of his influence and was determined to put an end to any "resistance." He was taken into custody in May 1941 and assigned to Auschwitz as Number 16670. When a prisoner escaped in July, Commandant Fritsch lined up the entire block and randomly selected ten inmates to be put to death as payback for the escapee. According to Fritsch, they were ordered into a bunker and left without food or water until they "dried up like tulip bulbs." Among the doomed men was Sergeant Francis Gajowniczek, who whispered, to no one in particular: "My poor wife and children." Kolbe came forward and offered to replace the sergeant, stating that he had no family. On July 31, Kolbe and the other nine were taken into custody; by August 14, all save Kolbe and three other inmates who were unconscious had passed away. An orderly was dispatched to administer a carbolic acid injection to end their lives.

The Nagais were not aware of any of this because of the news blackout. But occasionally, when Midori visited the Lourdes Grotto he constructed, she would think of Kolbe. Gran moistened the dying doctor's lips with water from the shrine without mentioning Kolbe. No one else in the room did either. Nagai was certain that Kolbe's prayers were the reason for the recovery. Kolbe was not then a well-known saint who had been declared a saint. However, the majority of Christians who travel to Nagasaki on pilgrimage today stop at both

Nagai's hut and Kolbe's shrine. It is fitting since, in some way, the horrifying hues of the Auschwitz and Nagasaki fires were collected and changed into pure light as they passed through these two men's hearts.

Not from Chance Our Comfort Springs

After Nagai's incredible recovery on October 5, government medical personnel took over, allowing the band to go back to their own residences. Nagai prayed for Midori and the other deceased from the university hospital during a time of sadness. He lived as penitentially as he could at the time, according to an ancient Eastern custom of not shaving his beard or hair. He also went back to Urakami during this time to address the issue of lingering radiation. He didn't have any tools, but he was certain that the fallout had been mostly washed away by the autumn rains when he found live ants and subsequently earthworms. There was no truth to the outlandish rumors that life would cease to exist for seventy years. Back to work, like the ants! Leaning charred beams against his home's stone retaining wall and covering the roof with pieces of heat-buckled tin, he constructed a modest hut with the assistance of some pals. His kids moved in with Gran after demanding to live with their father. While 8,000 Catholics perished in Urakami, others were either abroad in the army or in Japanese colonies at the time of the bombing. Many people built shelters around Nagai's house in response to his call to reconstruct the area. Nagai participated enthusiastically in the planning of a new university by returning to the area where Midori and 8,000 Christians perished "so that I could contemplate the meaning of the event." Some were whispering that the A-bomb was clearly heaven's punishment, or tenbatsu. The bishop invited Nagai to speak on behalf of the laity at this point and announced plans for an outdoor Mass for the deceased. Nagai stepped up his search for the A-bomb's significance. He came to a stunning realization after thinking back on two incidents. Around midnight following the bombing, Nurse Kosasa and a few other radiology staff heard women singing Latin hymns. When they passed the location the following morning, they found the nearly nude bodies of twenty-seven nuns from Josei Convent, but they were too tired to give it much thought. The convent had been destroyed by the explosion, which also left some nuns terribly burned and murdered others. These latter, who were gathered around a little adjacent brook, clearly suffered from torment, but they passed away singing!

The other event involved girls from Junshin, a school managed by nuns that Nagai was familiar with and where Midori had taught. Sister Ezumi, the administrator, ordered the entire school to perform a song daily for God's protection as the air strikes become more frequent. It began with the words, "Mary, Mother! I give my entire being—body, soul, and spirit—to you. The girls came to sing it with great earnestness during the extremely sad days of 1945. Many Junshin females were working in factories in Tokitsu and Michino on the morning of August 9. While some died instantaneously, others endured severe burns from infrared radiation, were slashed by flying glass or roofing iron, and experienced the awful thirst that A-bomb victims are known for. In the days and weeks that followed, Nagai heard several tales of small gatherings of Junshin girls by the river, in a field, or in a makeshift dispensary. Singing lines from their hymn, "Mother Mary, I offer myself to you," they continued to support one another despite the fact that the majority were seriously hurt and that many would die within days.

Inside the ruins of the church, Nagai was sitting on a mound of debris and reflecting over his remarks at the outdoor Mass. Charred timbers lying in a crisscross pattern in the waning light resembled the black limbs of winter plum trees—black, like the sun in the Book of Revelation and the rain and the sun on August 9! He looked at the shattered altar—the killed Lamb! Everywhere the Lamb of Revelation walked, he was accompanied "by a white-robed choir of virgins singing."

Nagai understood what to say to the dejected, burned, hobbling, and bandaged Catholics who gathered around the broken cathedral to help at a Requiem Mass for their deceased on November 23, 1945. He stood up a little unsteadily when it was his turn to talk, his gaunt features, uncut hair and beard like those of an ancient mountain shaman, the sennin.

"On the morning of August 9, a meeting of the Supreme Council of War was in session at Imperial Headquarters, Tokyo, to decide whether Japan would surrender or continue to wage war," he said, bowing slowly to the robed priests and then to the crowd. The planet was at a turning point at that very moment. A choice between further brutal bloodshed and carnage or peace had to be made. Then an atom bomb exploded over our suburb at 11:02 a.m. Immediately, 8,000 Christians were called to God, and within a few hours, this revered holy site in the Far East was reduced from flames to ash. That night, at midnight, our cathedral unexpectedly caught fire and burned to ashes. His Majesty the Emperor announced his sacred decision to terminate the war in the Imperial Palace at precisely that moment. The world witnessed peace when the Imperial Rescript, which officially ended the battle, was promulgated on August 15. The great feast of the Virgin Mary's Assumption falls on August 15. I think the dedication of the Urakami Cathedral to her is important. It is important to consider if the war's conclusion and her feast day celebration were the result of God's enigmatic Providence or whether they were just coincidental.

I've heard that another city was supposed to receive the atom bomb. The American crew made their way to Nagasaki, the secondary target, after heavy clouds made that goal impracticable. The bomb was dropped more north than intended due to a mechanical issue, and it exploded directly above the cathedral. I don't think our suburb was selected by the American crew. Urakami was selected by God's Providence, and the bomb passed directly over our houses. Is there not a significant connection between the war's conclusion and the destruction of Nagasaki? During World War II, was Nagasaki not the lamb without a blemish, the lamb selected to atone for the sins of all the countries by being killed as a whole and burned on an altar of sacrifice?

The Japanese term for the Bible's "holocaust," or full burnt offering, was hansai, which Nagai utilized. The most current film about Nagai's life, Children of Nagasaki, by renowned director Keisuke Kinoshita, effectively captures the irate response of some mourners. In response, a few members of the congregation got up and yelled that Nagai ought to attempt to use religious language to elevate the horror that was done to their families! Nagai was neither surprised nor angry. He understood their reaction since he had been through the dark valley they were in. With a gentle power that demanded stillness, he went on.

Nagai resorted to the poetry of the Easter Vigil, a yearly ritual held in the cathedral during which the tall Paschal Candle is ignited in the predawn darkness. "That holocaust on August 9 at midnight, when flames rose from the cathedral, banishing darkness and bringing the light of peace, was so noble and magnificent." We were able to look up at something lovely, pure, and divine even in the midst of our sorrow!

Nagai concluded by pointing to the skull-shaped hill outside of Jerusalem and the Mount of the Beatitudes: "Happy are those who weep; they shall be comforted." We must tread the path of reparation—being scolded, thrashed, and subjected to bleeding, sweaty punishment for our transgressions. We can, however, focus on Jesus bearing his Cross up the Calvary hill. It has been given by the

Lord and taken away by him. The Lord's name is blessed. We should be grateful that Nagasaki was selected to receive the entire charred sacrifice! Let us express gratitude for the world's peace and Japan's religious freedom as a result of this sacrifice. There was a profound hush after Nagai finished and sat down. The listeners were profoundly affected by his discovery of God's Providence at work even in the horrors of August 9, and non-Christians in Nagasaki and throughout Japan were also profoundly affected when he repeated this discovery later in his writings.

Nagai took up residence in his small cabin, which was not impervious to wind, rain, or snow, as the winter quickly demonstrated. He was expected to live for two to three years, according to the most recent medical assessment. His children, a ten-year-old son and a four-year-old daughter, were his top priority. In an effort to "educate them in self-reliance," he was committed to spending as much time with them as he could. Only those who were self-sufficient would survive in a society and economy shattered by the catastrophic conflict. They would learn in this rudimentary shelter. Gran, who was still too numb to protest, had just accepted his ideas once he had told her about them. Their initial kitchen consisted of an open fireplace, an iron pot without a handle, and an earthenware jar with a broken neck as utensils.

They were joined by two relatives who had nowhere else to go. They had to switch places in the "bed" each night, with the first head at the north end, the second at the south, and so on, in order to accommodate the six within. They just had blankets, by the way, and sleeping in this manner helped them stay warm. The bomb had taken away all of their bedding and most of their clothing. Even though winter arrived with snow and rain, they avoided getting colds. This was an unanticipated advantage of Urakami's radiation dosage, according to Nagai. Radiation-exposed wheat was sprouting rapidly everywhere, he had seen. Similarly, corn sprouted but produced no grain. Immediately after the blast, morning glories produced new tendrils, but the leaves were distorted and the flowers were tiny. Sweet potatoes blossomed quite instantly but yielded no crop, whereas green veggies flourished.

Professor Suetsugu, who is currently employed at the esteemed Kyoto University's x-ray department, stopped over to visit his former colleague who had succeeded him as dean of Nagasaki. The hut was the only place Nagai could meet him. The tokonoma is used by any cultured Japanese householder to invite guests inside the room. Above a barely raised pedestal, this tall but narrow alcove is half-framed by an unpainted cypress beam that shows its natural grain. A hanging scroll with calligraphy or a brief poem from classical Chinese literature is typically seen inside the alcove. Suetsugu pulled out a brush and drew a traditional Chinese poetry on a piece of white paper, even though Nagai's one-room hut lacked a floor, let alone a tokonoma: Butsu dokoro mu jin zo mu ichi! There is nothing here, but it is an infinite treasury! Nagai was overjoyed. He had been telling his kids the exact same thing. The poem, which he affixed to the wall, held greater significance for him than the exquisite tokonoma and ancient scrolls in their former residence.

A local well was providing water to an elderly guy. He had to put the bucket to the bottom and struggle to gather water because the explosion had thrown in a lot of debris. Nagai told his son Makoto, "See that, son." That is how our lives are now. We're just getting started. We must start with virtually nothing and lay the groundwork in the dark. But, boy, if we have faith and patience, we can succeed. God is with us.

Later, Nagai caught sight of a young acquaintance staring blankly at the nuclear wasteland. When he was enlisted into the Marines a few years prior, he was among the youngest members of Saint Vincent de Paul. In a raggedy remnant that was long out of food and medicine, he fought a rearguard action in the South Pacific jungles to end the war. He had to summon all his strength to avoid lying down in the jungle muck and allowing the malaria to lull him into merciful slumber. He persevered because he believed that his parents needed him. Now that he was back in Urakami, he learned that his parents had mysteriously passed away on August 9. He sobbed like a child as he sat on a scorched rock close to where his house used to be. Without saying anything, Nagai, who had been observing him, moved to his side and wrapped an arm over him. The emaciated former soldier remarked, "I endured a lot in the jungle, but I persisted for them," as the shoulders ceased to tremble. All I've gone through is pointless now that they're dead! I want to leave this place and move so far away that I won't be reminded of Urakami ever again. "Yes," Nagai replied, "I can appreciate that emotion. However, their deaths and all of your suffering will mean little to you if you leave and forget. You can preserve their names and give your sorrows a great deal of significance if you remain in Urakami and construct a cabin similar to ours. In place of the old house, the young man stayed and constructed a hut. A year later, he introduced his future bride to Nagai and bowed low.

Nagai started his first book in pencil because it was difficult to get pen and ink. His findings and experiences treating A-bomb patients in the month after August 9 were documented in a 100-page medical study. In order to assist medical professionals in treating the numerous victims who were still suffering in Nagasaki and Hiroshima, he wrote the first scientific explanation of the effects of an A-bomb. His work turned out to be a true contribution to medical knowledge, and it had the advantage of being written by a radiation specialist who had received a double dosage himself.

A number of acquaintances approached Nagai and offered to help him and his kids by finding him a suitable wife from the numerous battle widows. Nagai considered this carefully but declined. "It is a terrible thing for a child to lose a mother, far worse than losing a father," he said as his justification. Both of my kids have lovely recollections of Midori. They would become much more perplexed if a stepmother were introduced into their lives. Personal consideration was another factor. His children, particularly his daughter, bore a striking resemblance to their mother. He wrote while Kayano was by his side, but he would never be able to forget Midori or consider picking a different Mrs. Nagai.

He concluded that a popular book about the A-bomb was needed in Japan. On Christmas Eve 1945, with the assistance of a friend, Ichitaro Yamada, he came up with the main idea and the title. The Urakami Cathedral had two bell towers before to August, each with a matching cupola that held two large bells. The A-bomb flung the cupola on the north, or left-hand, side scores of yards away. In the bank of the little stream next to the cathedral, a portion of it is still discernible. Its bell was irreparably shattered. Tons of brick, masonry, burnt girders, and ash smothered the southern cupola, which fell straight down with the bell.

Yamada was on a nearby island as a soldier when the A-bomb was dropped. Upon his hasty return to Urakami, he found that his parents, his five children, and his wife had all been physically destroyed by the explosion. In a state of near despair, he visited his friend Nagai. He needed to express his rage to someone. After his outburst, Yamada listened to Nagai because he understood the depth of the wound caused by Midori's passing. According to Nagai, the only option available to everyone who accepted the gospel was to view the A-bomb as a component of God's Providence, which always results in good out of evil. Nagai grinned and added, "Let's climb the Mount of the Beatitudes together." Yamada means "mountain field." Nagai took the broken Yamada as a disciple. The two concluded that it may be worthwhile to dig for the buried bell when December arrived. By the late hours of December 24, Yamada and a few young guys had cleared the mound of debris and were able to view the top of the bell. Nagai lead them in the Rosary while they were eating lunch. After that, they resolutely cleared the bell's sides and looked for any flaws. When Yamada raised the bell and set up block and tackle, it appeared to be sound. When it was nearly six in the morning and the bell was safely dangling from a tripod of cypress logs, they made the decision to ring the Angelus.

Unaware of whether the buried bell would ring, Nagai, Yamada, and their assistants had not told the Urakami Christians about their effort. With nothing to look forward to but the dullest midnight Mass ever in a burnt-out hall of Saint Francis Hospital, the latter were currently sitting down for scanty suppers in drafty shelters. The winter darkness was abruptly changed by a true miracle. The sentimental Angelus! The lack of big buildings in the hut suburb made the peals all the more obvious. They believed that the cathedral had risen from the ashes to celebrate the birth of Christ. Like the shepherds, they listened in wonder as the song emanated from the pitch-black heavens over Bethlehem. The Bells of Nagasaki, the title of Nagai's novel, was born that night. Its message would be that God's bells cannot be silenced, not even by an A-bomb.

Although there was a shortage of paper and even fewer places to write, the book slowly came into being. As he wrote, he started to consider himself as the voice of the 72,000 people who died in Nagasaki, as well as the widows, widowers, and orphans they left behind. The book is written in layman's terms but provides an objective scientific overview of the A-bomb. He uses a lot of straightforward yet powerful stories, such as this one: "It is nighttime, and I am in bed in the hut with four-year-old Kayano in my arms." She reflexively goes beneath my shirt and grabs my nipple even though she is sleepy and nearly asleep. She shudders when she recognizes that it is not her mother's breast and that she has vanished. She is suddenly awake and crying.

He would go deeper into the complex issue of atomic energy in subsequent volumes. "Atomic energy is a secret that God placed within the universe," he asks simply in this book. This secret has been revealed by scientists. Will civilization advance tremendously as a result of this, or will it destroy our planet? Is atomic energy essential for surviving or for annihilation? Genuine religion, in my opinion, is the only source of guidance for applying this key.

Real religion? What do you think of it? In the radioactive wilderness, Nagai describes how he and his small community found religious hope. On the final page of his book, he kneels with his kids to recite the Angelus as the valley of ashes is filled with melody from the cathedral bell. They know that God is love, that suffering is meaningful, and that it is worth the effort to continue loving despite their loss and poverty. "Those who lack a vision die." Nagai has realized that the vision comes from prayer.

The actual Nihon-teki Nagai, a samurai descendent and admirer of Far Eastern classics, has united with the very French Pascal in their love of literature and science, but most importantly, in their understanding of prayer. For both of them, Psalm 36 said, "In your light we see light."

The Little Girl Who Could Not Cry

Kayano, Nagai's lively little daughter, subconsciously tried to ease the loneliness and worry of a child without a mother. One of the issues was that she was quite fond of her father. One day, Nagai's physician remarked: "Look, your spleen will burst if she just runs in and jumps on you." You know you have to prevent her from being overly friendly, so that would kill you! In Nyokodo, Nagai regrettably built a little barricade next to his bed. He was sleeping one day when she crept in next to him, leaned over, and kissed him. Now, pretending to sleep, he was awake and heard her murmur: "Ah! The sweet scent of my father. Nagai continues, "You may think that a man with leukemia is cold-blooded, but when I heard that pitiful cry, my blood ran hot through my veins. In my fantasy, I imagined little Kayano, who was now motherless and fatherless, returning home from my burial and burying her face in my mattress for a final "smell of my daddy," knowing that my death couldn't be far off.

As more people visited Nagai during the day, it became busier. After reading an article written by him or about him, people would come to this holy man for advice on a personal issue. Many were non-Christians, and some traveled from as far away as Tokyo and beyond. He was waking up at around two in the morning, anxious, even though his days were getting busier by the day. He was nearing the end of the two or three years the doctors had allotted him. What impact would his passing have on his kids? In the hopes that it might be helpful when they could comprehend, he made the decision to put what he wanted to say in writing. Two best-selling novels were to be written from these musings. The forty-year-old Nagai's mental patterns can be inferred from a brief synopsis.

"You are young children and have already lost your mother," he wrote.

That loss cannot be replaced. The loss of a mother is far worse than the death of a father. You will be left unprotected and alone in the world as orphans after my death. You'll cry. Yes, you may even cry uncontrollably, and that's okay as long as you do it in front of your heavenly father. "Happy are those who weep, for they shall be comforted" is a statement we have on the authority of his Son, and I have personally witnessed its validity. He will always wipe away your tears if you spill them in front of him. It is the Sermon on the Mount, where all the solutions are found. It can be challenging to climb this mountain, sometimes in snow, rain, and mist. But what a sight of love, serenity, and beauty when the clouds and mists clear! Yes, a view of the principles that endure, give our lives purpose, and make our hardships worthwhile. The only material belonging to me at the moment is this Nyokodo hut. Oh! Jesus, however, instructs us to love our eternal selves more than our worldly belongings. Indeed, we are all children of the Almighty Father! That makes us very valuable. Do you know that in your father's eyes, you are more valuable than the sun, the lovely, bright star that sustains our planet? Like everyone else around you, you are his own son and daughter. You will find serenity if you love everyone and have faith in his Providence. I can tell you that it is because I have tried it. My children, I have to tell you the truth. As orphans, you shall sip from a bitter chalice. You will have to resist the subtle urge to cynically abandon yourself to that gloomy and depressing unbelief known as fatalism, as well as the inclination to harbor hatred toward your school friends who have parents.

Live a meaningful and loving life and experience the Father's personal Providence instead of living a life that is negatively impacted by blind fate. He has requested that the three of us take a bitter beverage. When Jesus spoke of the sparrows that are precious in the Father's eyes and the lilies of the field, he was describing our "way" to peace and our involvement in his grand plan. As a physician, I occasionally had to provide bitter medication. I didn't say: What a miserable child! We ought to provide him some sugary drink! Don't you understand that? We believe in a wonderful God who provides us with the feeding, healing, and cleaning waters of life rather than giving us cheap syrup. Because of our poor taste, they can appear bitter at times. But keep going! He is preparing us to spend eternity in heaven with him and our loved ones. You've probably heard the story of the bluebird of happiness before. Unfortunately, your bluebird flew away after your mother passed away. Only in heaven will you be able to locate your bluebird again.

Nagai explained how evening will descend on Urakami's destroyed moonscape in a subsequent work, Rozario No Kusari (The Chain of the Rosary). Smoke would curl up from crude fireplaces, and lamps would glow from the shelters. At that point, he would start to think about Midori. He would want to cry because he would be so miserable. However, Kayano, his young daughter, never shed a tear! He would see her, just staring out at the radioactive devastation while chewing her lower lip as the sun set and darkness fell. Later, his brother Hajime's little daughter entered the room after waking up from a midday sleep, asking, "Where's kaa-chan [Mommy]?" with a confused expression. "In heaven," Kayano cleverly retorted. The confused child cried, "Kaa-chan," as she rushed into Hajime's wife as she entered. Nagai observed the clouding of Kayano's face. She approached the sliding paper door, or shoji, and simply stood there, running her finger along the panel frame. A pointless activity that holds great significance for him.

There was rubble and broken roof tiles scattered around the bleak waste surrounding their house. Kayano repeatedly stumbled and injured her knees, as Nagai witnessed. She would use her finger to gently rub the blood away, but she would never cry. She was once chased by an overly playful dog, and she fled inside Nagai's chamber in terror, not even letting forth a peep or a cry. This girl who was unable to weep disturbed him. It deepened and personalized his hate of the A-bomb and World War II. He hoped she would read it when she grew up since it inspired a written reflection in another book: Our ability to cry makes our childhood joyful. We are aware that our mother will come and console us if we cry. Since your mother passed away, Kayano, there have been moments when I wanted to cry uncontrollably. However, only a child with a mother can do it; an adult cannot. He goes on to say that when working in an orphanage, he observed that when an orphan cries, the other children laugh at them and teach them how to hold back their tears. "Happy are those who weep, for they shall be comforted," he says, the only person with the complete response. You may always cry in front of him, and he will listen to you.

Several of Nagai's favorite scientists—Pascal, Copernicus, Mendel, Pasteur, Ampere, and Marconi—are referenced in his writings. He stated, "These were the free men, who looked with humility and understanding at creation." The idea that faith and science were mutually exclusive irritated him much. He writes: "It isn't true if you read what the great scientists actually said." That assertion is made by social and literary commentators, or guys who have wielded pens but never test tubes. "One must approach the study of any part of God's creation with profound respect and a certain chastity," he continued, a little later in the book. A monk in his cell is truly at one with a true scientist conducting experiments in his lab. Indeed, experiments turn become prayers.

"A particular chastity." Nagai had a profound passion for science, particularly radiology and the study of atoms and radiation. The evidence was evident when he gladly bid farewell to the lecture halls where he had relished his celebrity position and relinquished his university and laboratory without bitterness. With no bitterness toward God or the Americans, he also bid farewell to Midori. Yes, tears and sadness, but no resentment. If you read his books or talk to others who knew him well, this becomes quite evident. The man they depicted "cared and did not care."

Nagai frequently discussed the sky and constellations in his writing. He never grew weary of their beauty, nor did he grow weary of the order and dependability that made them the essential companions of old land and sea travelers. Another love that lasted a lifetime was the mountains. They remained steadfast, protecting their massive cedar and cypress stands from summer heat, winter snow, and fall typhoons. The mountains, like as Fuji, Yakumo, Hiei, and Koya, were the traditional locations where his people had gained profound spiritual ideals, and he had always found tranquility there. However, one mountain—the Mount of the Beatitudes—becomes increasingly significant in his writing. "Being pure in heart and poor in spirit may not bring you a lot of money, but it will bring you something even more valuable, peace of heart," he said in a book he authored for his kids. When presents poured in from his readers, he would reiterate this to them and then share them with the entire impoverished neighborhood.

He describes an encounter with Kayano, age six, that greatly inspired him. Yamazato Primary School, which was only a hundred yards from her house, was where she had recently begun attending. Even though school had ended for about thirty minutes one day, she had not yet returned home. He was starting to get anxious when he heard little shuffling noises. She materialized in front of him with a cup in both hands, as though it held a priceless flame that could never go out. She went up onto his tatami floor, kicking off her shoes as though they didn't matter. Until she placed the cup on a shelf, her gaze remained fixed on it. Then she let out a loud sigh of relief. He asked her what it was, intrigued. The child grinned broadly and gave an explanation. According to Nagai, "everyone at school was given a cup of something new called pineapple juice that day." She decided it would help her ailing father because it tasted so sweet when she sipped it. She kept it under wraps until school let out, and as she was leaving, a seven-year-old bumped into her, spilling some. But after that, she didn't lose another drop. As she presented the cup with the remaining juice to him gravely, his eyes became wet.

Physically, their early days in the hut were a misery. Water crept in when it rained, making it difficult to make a fire outdoors and cook over it. The raw north wind joined them later in the year when snow arrived. Usually, hunger was an unwanted visitor to their temporary table. One night, Nagai grabbed a rat, which he cleaned and prepared since he knew it would provide protein. He learned that the old Japanese saying, "To an empty stomach, all food is tasty," is true. But things progressively got better, particularly after the carpenters constructed Nyokodo, his new home.

The friendship between the general and the Emperor played a significant role in the American shogun MacArthur's ability to orchestrate one of the most tranquil military occupations in history. The Japanese people supported MacArthur's reforms because they were intended to firmly establish democracy in Japanese society, prevent a return to militarism, and rebuild a damaged economy. He still had a strong hold on the media, though. MacArthur's censorship agency turned down a publisher's request to print The Bells of

Nagasaki after it was accepted. The A-bomb now caused the Americans to become sensitive. A question was starting to be asked around the world: Should Allied atrocities like the A-bomb not be held accountable if Nazis and Japanese generals were put to death for war crimes? Permission to print The Bells of Nagasaki was eventually granted in early 1949, on the condition that the book included an equivalent number of pages from the U.S. military court's documentation of Japanese crimes in the Philippines. After Nagai agreed to this clause, the book was published in tandem on April 1, 1949.

The Bells of Nagasaki was an instant hit, and a year later, a leading film studio, Shochiku, started making a movie adaptation that would go on to become a huge hit throughout Japan. Psychologically, the Japanese were prepared for a tale of a man who had lost everything during the war but still harbored optimism and even excitement for what was ahead. Many people could relate to Nagai's traumatic experiences. 2,470,000 Japanese people died between the start of the full-scale war in China in 1937 and the arrival of peace on August 15, 1945. Of them, 1,672,000 were killed in the armed forces, 289,000 were Japanese civilians in places like Manchuria, Korea, Okinawa, and so on, and 509,000 were killed in airstrikes on Japan itself. A total of 2.5 million people have died! In addition to being injured and having their houses, belongings, and means of subsistence destroyed, the majority of Japanese had experienced the death of a friend, family member, or relative. The morale was low and the future appeared dismal. Despite having lost nearly everything, Nagai was here, positively hopeful about life.

at an attempt to capture the essence of the bedridden Nagai and his wife Midori, the Shochiku Movie Company dispatched producer Hideo Oba along with the two main actors, Masao Wakahara and

Yumeji Tsukioka, to interview him at Nyokodo. The Bells of Nagasaki was the title given to the film. Hachiro Sato wrote a song for the film with the same name, which went on to become one of the decade's most enduring songs. Several well-known songbooks still include it. Like Ignatius of Loyola, the Japanese are extremely sentimental and believe that tears are a gift. The enormous audiences that saw The Bells of Nagasaki were exceptionally talented on this score!

Nagai wrote 20 books between the conclusion of the war in 1945 and his death in 1951, several of which were best sellers. Nyokodo Zuihitsu was one of the later (Reflections from Nyokodo). Because he produced this work in reaction to the 1950 conflict between North and South Korea, which involved United Nations forces, it contains more melancholy and more discussion of peace and the nuclear danger. Prior to 1950, he had written extensively about war and peace, but the Korean War added a crisis note to this book. Nagai passed away eighteen months before to the detonation of the H-bomb, which set off the major nuclear weapons controversy. Nonetheless, he wrote about the terrifying scope of nuclear war as well as the potential of atomic energy. His thoughts are worth remembering.

First of all, he never thought that the discovery of atomic energy would be the end of the world. He believed that the universe was good in its entirety and that atomic energy was just one aspect of its amazing dynamic. For example, the sun's warmth and light reached the planet through atomic energy. Using their cunning, our distant ancestors extracted the secret of fire from sticks and flint. The discovery of atomic energy was a "providential" development at a time when the world's oil reserves were running low. Naturally, just as with fire, oil, electricity, and dynamite, human responsibility was required. Atomic energy made living with risk and uncertainty much more painful and increased the dangers significantly, although these factors have always accompanied humanity on its historical journey. Risk and suffering even appear to be essential to our development as fully human beings—that is, mature, complex, and compassionate individuals.

Since Japan's complete scarcity of oil was the primary cause of his nation's war with America, Nagai was especially aware of this issue. He believed that Japan's long-standing energy issue might be resolved by atomic energy. He passed away before this became a reality, but soon there were more and more nuclear power plants all around the country. The majority of Japanese people think that the 1941 condition of depending on imported fuel was even scarier than the dangers of nuclear power.

Nagai harbored the fervent faith that the terrible nature of A-bombs would prevent the superpowers from going to war with one another until the Korean War broke out in 1950. That illusion was shattered by the Korean War, which came as such a shock and disappointment that, in spite of his dreadful physical state, he felt obliged to start writing another significant book. His enlarged spleen was pushing his heart out of position, he was experiencing frequent fevers, and he was experiencing persistent bone discomfort. This later feature of his deteriorating illness was quite painful.

Nagai starts his new book by outlining basic historical facts on the conflict between the West and Communism that led to the Korean War. People's courts in the areas that the Soviet and Chinese troops controlled following World War II tried anti-Communists as "enemies of mankind," and many of them were put to death, imprisoned, or transferred to detention camps.

Only after the Hiroshima A-bomb, nine days prior to Japan's capitulation, did the Soviet army enter the war. In China and

Manchuria, the Russians captured every Japanese soldier they could find and imprisoned them in labor camps in Siberia. Hajime, Nagai's younger brother, who spent thirty months in one of these camps, described to Nagai the brutal treatment they endured and the number of people who died there. The Western Allies, on the other hand, sent Japanese soldiers home to civilian life. The small number of alleged war criminals who were tried in public tribunals and given defense attorneys were the sole exceptions. Readers drawn to the elegant theories of Communism were urged by Nagai to research contemporary world history and "judge the tree by its fruits." The anti-American or anti-Western sentiment that would later become a divisive feature of many "peace movements" was never present in Nagai's antiwar work.

Nagai had disturbing recollections of the decade leading up to the war in the Pacific, when fascist slogans were used to control Japanese rioters. He detested slogan-crying mobs because he believed they were superficial individuals who avoided doing the necessary research to comprehend the topics they were protesting. Additionally, he wrote scathing criticism of religious and political figures that "used" the desire for peace held by the average person. He believed that achieving world peace was both noble and difficult, and that politicians and ideologues were reckless for promising easy fixes at low cost.

He had serious misgivings over "angry people" in peace campaigns. He wrote that peace movements are desperately needed, but only if they are composed of people who have peaceful souls. Any peace movement that was "merely political" or dogmatic and uncommitted to justice, love, and patient labor should be avoided, he said. He remarked that angry yelling about peace in the streets frequently betrays extremely unpeaceful souls. His writing did not make him popular with everyone!

The aforementioned is not very noteworthy, but he was noteworthy for advocating for the Sermon on the Mount as the workable blueprint for global peace. He adds that a Christian will not insist on the Communist laying down his sickle before attempting to make peace with him. Even if it means getting wounded by that sickle, the Christian will hug the Communist without a weapon. Completely unworkable? "Yes," he says, "unless you know how to pray." However, other people believe that praying is "plain superstition" or "no different from purchasing a lottery ticket," thus it's not really any form of prayer. "Going off to mountains alone and becoming ascetics" is not a requirement of true prayer. No, as soon as we are able to communicate with the loving One who is the origin of all dynamism in the universe, we can begin to pray. According to Nagai, we are all invited to contemplation, "which is not difficult." For example, around Christmas, you witness kids praying in this manner in front of the crib. "I thank you, Father, for revealing these things to little ones and hiding them from the clever," he says, quoting the Gospel. He continues, "All of us are called to become little ones, and little ones can discover the delightful wellsprings of contemplation!" The invitation from the gospel is for everyone to reflect.

The Cloud of Unknowing, written by a fourteenth-century English mystic, is a well-known work on Christian reflection. In order to encounter the God of revelation, Moses must ascend into the shadows of Mount Sinai, which is covered in clouds. Nagai tasted reflection in a mushroom cloud that was darkened by a nuclear desert. "I have learned the depths of God's friendship by walking with him through Urakami's nuclear wasteland," he wrote. For many, the mushroom cloud represents hopelessness and the end of the world. By guiding the people away from the scientific servitude of a new Egypt, Nagai's faith turned it into the cloud of another Exodus. The beauty of Zion was first realized after Jerusalem was destroyed and its inhabitants were taken as prisoners to Babylon. With the confidence of Isaiah, Nagai gazed out over the radioactive wasteland and declared: "God will turn [Jerusalem's] desolation into Eden, and the wasteland into a garden of Yahweh."

Japanese Zen expert William Johnston has had a significant influence on the discourse between Buddhist Japan and the (sometimes) Christian West. He thinks Nagai made a significant addition to his specialty, which is Buddhist and Christian prayer experiences. "Nagai the scientist, Nagai the patriot, Nagai the humanist became Nagai the mystic," Johnston says in the preface of his English translation of Nagai's first widely read work, The Bells of Nagasaki. He is a contemporary mystic of peace. He has a special position in the enormous amount of atomic literature. He makes an effort at a theology that is the result of terrible sorrow and heartbreaking conversion. He holds a revered position next to renowned prophets with his message of love.

The woman he loved was reduced to burnt bones by the obscene mushroom cloud. However, his belief in God's providence transformed the malevolent fission flames into Elijah's enigmatic chariot. Two Chinese ink paintings he created while resting in Nyokodo make this very evident. The modest Nagai Museum, which presently sits next to the hut, has them on display.

Murillo's depiction of the Blessed Virgin Mary ascending into heaven on a cloud is clearly the model for the first painting, which features Mary. The second is comparable, except Midori is the woman above the cloud. She is not as elegantly dressed as Mary; instead, she is wearing the loose-fitting blouse and wartime uniform that she was wearing when the A-bomb detonated over Urakami. Another distinction is that Midori is perched above a mushroom cloud.

The Song of a Tokyo Leper

Nagai was being read throughout Japan by the end of 1948. On May 25, 1949, his book Kono Ko wo Nokoshite received special recognition from the National Welfare Ministry. The National Education Ministry included portions concerning Nagai to textbooks and suggested that all schools watch the movie The Bells of Nagasaki when it was released. He was also well-known abroad. The first book written in English by a nuclear bomb survivor was Nagai's collection of stories titled We of Nagasaki. He started receiving gifts from readers in North and South America. Four more Nagai books were released in fast succession, and more magazines carried pieces about the dying scientist who continued to write and work.

A fairly unusual bill was introduced in the Japanese National Diet's Lower House in September 1949. It suggested that two Japanese, physicist Hideki Yukawa, Japan's first Nobel laureate, and scientist Takashi Nagai, the holy man of Nagasaki, be honored for their significant contributions to reviving the nation. The bill was opposed by left-socialist and communist Diet members. Although they acknowledged Yukawa's qualifications, they vehemently objected to any praise of the "religious sentimentalist" Nagai from the Diet. The campaign shifted to demonization: Nagai didn't actually have radiation sickness or even suffer from an A-bomb injury! In an attempt to get a fast payday, he used a ghostwriter to write the books and articles that were published under his name rather than writing them himself. Media outlets were available to anti-Nagai politicians, who dishonestly used them to prevent the Christian Nagai from being hailed as a national hero.

Friends of Nagai, like as historian Kataoka, were incensed and pleaded with him to refute the accusations made in public. Nagai declined for reasons they could not understand. Despite his obvious pain, he said, "Let it be." Since every idea in my publications comes from the Bible or other individuals, they are fundamentally correct when they claim that I haven't written the books. I also don't pretend to be a great writer. All of my writing motivation comes from God's grace. However, Japan's prime minister lacked Nagai's humility and patience. This was Shigeru Yoshida, who before to the war had made a name for himself as a foreign ambassador. He fiercely opposed Japan's new militarists when serving as ambassador to Great Britain before the war, a country he greatly respected for its traditions and legal system. He was imprisoned in Tokyo prior to the end of the war, compelled to leave his position by the latter, and sat out the war in Japan. He served as prime minister for seven years following the war and was vocally pro-Western and liberal. He detested Japanese Communists, whom he claimed were trying to destroy Japan in the name of a foreign philosophy. He had a suspicion that Nagai's Christian beliefs was the sole reason the Communists attacked him. Despite not being a Christian, Yoshida held the Sacred Heart sisters in great regard, and they educated his daughter as well as the daughters of other of his diplomatic colleagues in Japan and abroad. A Diet committee was established by Yoshida to look into the accusations made against Nagai.

The chairman of the committee visited Nagasaki and conducted interviews with Nagai's publishers, university employees, physicians, and city authorities. He even studied book manuscripts that Nagai painstakingly penciled. Editors from magazines stepped up and showed the chairman the pointless articles Nagai had authored. Nagai the radiologist's case history of Nagai's leukemia was originally recorded by Assistant Professor Asanaga of Nagasaki Medical University: Nagai had been employed as a pioneer with an x-ray facility without a radiation barrier for a year starting in 1932. Nagai x-rayed for eight hours a day and more between 1934 and 1937, when medical professionals were still unsure of how much radiation they could take in without running the risk of developing leukemia. In addition to his busy routine of x-rays with hospital patients and medical students, he pioneered and continued to lead the hospital's tuberculosis detection section from 1940 to 1945, x-raying a large number of people after the war had depleted the radiology workforce. Asanaga contributed a thorough diagnostic of Nagai's chronic leukemia due to radiation exposure following the A-bomb, indicating that Nagai was almost certain to develop radiation cancer.

The general public also started to defend Nagai after hearing his encouraging responses to their distressing correspondence. The museum at Nyokodo still has bundles of this letter. In 1985, when visiting a sick friend in Tokyo's western district, I met one of Nagai's "pen pals." He was in a facility for people with Hansen's illness who had stabilized. We were talking when Matron Koseki entered the room and inquired as to why I was in Tokyo. When I informed her that I was gathering information about Dr. Nagai, she responded right away. "Dr. Nagai? Really? Oh, hold on a second.

I was left perplexed as she hurried away, but she quickly came back with a note. She told me the scenario and said, "Look, this is Dr. Nagai's response to a letter I wrote." She was employed as a nurse in a government leprosarium in 1949. A nurse's responsibilities back then included reading books to patients who had Hansen's disease, which frequently caused blindness. She somehow got her hands on a Nagai book. She responded to the author after reading it to her patients, expressing "how beautiful it was to see hot tears running from their sightless eyes." With the letter she was holding in her hand, he responded. One of its waka poems, "Hito ni torite totoki mono wa tamashi to Shirashimen tame ni rai wa aru nari," could have sparked intense animosity if it had been written by someone else.

The low table we were sitting at on the tatami floor was thudded by my blind friend, Hihara-san. "That's correct, exactly. When I got leprosy, I was a young, naive man with a lovely wife and daughter. I was banished to a moat-guarded leper colony, shunned by society, and shunned by my wife and daughter. I gave up and tried to end my life. Here was Nagai, however, who had lost everything, was dying, and was content with both the world and himself. Nagai started writing to us after the matron continued to read to us. He brought me to the faith that finds that everything in life is a gift and a grace, and to Christ. Now that I've been a leper for fifty years, I can say, "Thank God for Nagai and thank God for my leprosy."

After the Nagai investigation group returned to Tokyo on December 23, 1949, the National Diet decided to declare Nagai a national hero. The governor of Nagasaki Prefecture and the city's mayor accompanied the state minister in Nyokodo to deliver the presentation. For the occasion, the Emperor sent Nagai three cups of silver sake, something he had never done before.

In December 1949, Nagai received even another award when he was named Nagasaki's first honorary citizen. When Nagai was informed of this, according to his friend Professor Kataoka, he uttered the following statement without showing any emotion: "The moon that illuminates the night sky is nothing more than a frigid ball of substance reflecting the sun's light! This honorary citizenship is nothing more than a manifestation of God's light. You know I don't have any illusions about myself. I would be that worthless servant mentioned in the Gospels if it weren't for God.

Yamazato Primary School is less than five minutes away from Nagai's hut. Of its 1,100 students, nine hundred died in the A-bomb explosion. Many of them had perished in the playground, where a white granite monument was placed when the school was restored. The image of a young girl surrounded by fire is engraved in bronze on the granite. Her hands are clasped together in prayer, and her countenance is calm. They asked Nagai to write an inscription.Every year on August 9, the school gathers solemnly to remember the tragedy, and the poem is performed to an eerie tune. Leading Japanese composers set several of Nagai's poetry to music, the most well-known being Kosaku Yamada, who is renowned throughout Japan (and beyond) for his incredibly poignant composition Aka Tomba (Red dragonfly).

The Navel of the World

Nagai makes it a point to identify with the lepers of Tokyo's Zenshoen in his letters to them. He starts one letter by saying, "My body too is breaking up." Yes, it's nearly finished. However, going through physical pain is a chance to collect riches for heaven. After just a few years of sincere effort bearing our burdens—and everyone has them—we will rise again and experience pure delight. "I was deeply moved to know that you are praying for me," reads another letter. How wonderful it is to know that God's love is what has motivated our correspondence and support for one another. For these leper buddies he had never met, Nagai wrote several tanka poems. Your spirits are robust, bright, and eternal, even though the body cries out of your bones! Human brilliance is demonstrated here. Another reads: "Father Damien's body broke apart on the barren, windswept island of Molokai, and they buried what was left behind." However, he resides in Light. "Even though our bodies are done for, how much better off are we than if it were our hearts that were corrupting?" Nagai asks in another letter.

Despite his limitations, Nagai writes openly and humorously about them. If kids played around in the library he had constructed for them next to Nyokodo, he might get furious. He utilized the money from his writing to establish a small library where kids could learn because it had been nearly difficult to study in the early huts constructed at Urakami and books were scarce. After it was finished, he established certain strict guidelines regarding silence. Nyokodo would yell, "Be quiet or go home!" to terrify children who broke them. Though he would quickly regret taking himself too seriously, there were times when he too became caustic!

In an attempt to bring Christian Urakami back to life, Nagai was joined by Professor Kataoka, a friend from 1934 who had experienced the loss of his home and family on "that day." In 1962, Kataoka published a 366-page biography of Nagai and authored the introductions for several new editions of Nagai's works. (I have the eleventh printing of the latter.) According to Kataoka, Nagai blended delicate warmth with unwavering dedication: "I can't recall anyone who met him who wasn't captivated by the love that poured out of the man's every pore.... He had a great feeling of obligation to the people who came before us, who left us our culture and civilization, as well as to the people who will come after us, to whom we must pass on what we have both benefited from and strived to better. A genuine love and devotion for the human race was the source of this sense of obligation.

A person who is bedridden may become demanding, erratic, and self-centered. After six years of living near Nagai the sick, Kataoka observed that Nagai was free of that natural but annoying weakness. The longer Nagai's illness persisted, the more outgoing, grateful, and other-centered his novels and letters became. For example, his leper pals stated they eagerly anticipated his letters since they were "happy." "Sometimes I feel that if I write another page, I'll collapse with exhaustion," he wrote in a book he finished a month before his death. However, I complete it, and I'm eager to do more! In fact, I can write far more quickly now than I could when I was writing my doctoral thesis years ago. Then, out of need, I wrote. Like the biking team behind a long-distance runner, I had to keep telling myself to keep going. Like a boy doing what he enjoys, I write now. When a boy wakes up and notices that the day is sunny, he exclaims, "Wow, what a fantastic day for baseball." When he wakes up in the rain, he exclaims, "Wow, what a fantastic day for eel catching." There is a song called "Let's go to it" that is set to the type of music that males hear in their hearts, despite the fact that I am unable to leave my bed.

Some people produce haiku poetry as a source of income. Do you know what I believe? We ought to turn our livelihood into haiku poetry. You may work in a clattering factory, on a fishing boat that tosses, or struggling to make ends meet in a run-down store. In such unpoetic circumstances, there are individuals who have composed inspirational haiku poetry. And if we truly want it, we can turn any job and every hour of the day into a poetry. Naturally, we must first develop a heart that is both serious and playful! We must look past appearances, see the underlying beauty that exists everywhere, and appreciate the wonderful things that surround us. After that, every day turns into a haiku poem.

According to Nagai, the Sermon on the Mount is extremely "practical" and relevant to all facets of our existence. He claimed to have left college because he thought a doctor had the power to end a patient's life, but he later learned from his own medical experiences that God is ultimately in control of all life. He goes on: "Physicians should take the Sermon on the Mount's statement that "fortunate are those who weep" literally. A true physician endures pain alongside every patient. The doctor shares the patient's fear of dying. The doctor replies, "Thank you," when the patient finally recovers and says, "Thank you." You treat an elderly patient as if he were your own father, and a child as if he were your own child. Every patient becomes your mother, brother, or sister, and you sacrifice everything for them. Reexamining those tests and x-rays with anxiety, you go through the medical chart, looking everywhere. How naive I was as a young physician to believe that medical practice was solely a question of technique. A doctor would then be a body mechanic! No, a doctor needs to be someone who experiences all of the physical and emotional suffering that a patient endures. I now realize that practicing medicine is a vocation, a personal calling from God; therefore, administering an injection, taking an x-ray, or examining a patient are all aspects of God's kingdom. I started praying for every patient I saw after realizing that.

Nagai was equally at home with the scholarly affluent as he was with the ignorant poor, and they were with him, much like Francis of Assisi, whom he adored dearly. Scholars, farmers, believers, atheists, and Communists were among the diverse range of people who came to speak with this impoverished man from Nyokodo. Eva Peron, a former actress and the wife of the Argentinean dictator who came to power on the backs of "the shirtless ones," was one unique fan. She entrusted a Japanese ship's captain with a big statue of our Lady of Luhan, the patroness of Argentina, which she conveyed to Nagai. This delighted Japanese migrants in Brazil, who requested that the captain bring a second statue of Mary for the Nagasaki people. Watanabe, the ship's captain, transported the statues to Nagasaki by rail because the boat could only go as far as Kobe. He was greeted civically by prefectural and municipal officials at the station, where the flags of both countries proudly shook in the sea air. A vibrant procession led the two statues to Nagai's cottage, where they were placed in an open car decorated with flowers. Thirty Junshin nuns led the throng in singing Marian songs as they greeted the procession with lit candles. With the monument that Eva Peron had sent, Captain Watanabe entered Nyokodo and saluted. In order to kiss Mary's feet, Nagai urged him to move the base closer. After bidding Nagai farewell, the group proceeded in a torchlight procession to the cathedral. Now, Nagai and his religion were so ingrained in Nagasaki culture that civic officials who practiced Buddhism and Shinto found nothing strange about taking part in this open display of Catholic devotion.

Nagai had a certain joy of life that was characteristic of southern European saints like Francis of Assisi, Philip Neri, and Don Bosco. It may be seen in some of his drawings in Chinese ink, such as the one of the Urakami boys attending a catechism lesson. They are in different phases of long-suffering and inattention, and they are roughly ten years old. Some are watching the ceiling, while another is surreptitiously dropping a lemon drop into a friend's hand and blowing bubble gum. A quite ordinary boys' Bible class! A poem composed in the hilarious local dialect—a cockney-like patois that Nagasaki youths use among themselves—accompanies the drawing. The poem would read, in Australian vernacular: "Left Saint Augustine scratchin' 'is 'ead, it did; scratchin' is bloody 'ead." However, I was aware that it was fair. 1. There is only one God and three Persons. The humorous medium conveyed a difficult lesson that was at the heart of both Nagai's and Pascal's thinking: The mystery of God is beyond the realm of science and mathematics.

The non-believer who stands outside and makes negative judgments about the Mass is similar to an old-timer I know who lived in the highlands, Nagai wrote. Despite never having watched a film, he used to snarl about how young people today waste so much money on movie theaters! Like a lot of things in life, the Mass is experienced rather than articulated. It is not just understood in the intellect; it is experienced in the spirit. I had a spiritual experience of Calvary during the Mass. As I lay here in Nyokodo, motionless, you know what I miss more than anything else? going to Sunday Mass with my kids and Midori. I sometimes long for the time when I might visit the cathedral and have a conversation with Christ in the tabernacle.

The French poet who said that the hole excavated for the Cross on Mount Calvary became "the navel of the world" was praised by Nagai. Like many Japanese, Nagai had a particular fondness for this inconspicuous aspect of our anatomy and used it as the topic of several sketches and poems, such as the haiku for Nobel Prize laureate and physicist Hideki Yukawa, who visited him in Nyokodo. "One truth, one world, one navel in the center of our belly," it said. Despite the English term "navel gazing," the navel is not a sign of self-preoccupation for Buddhists or Nagai. The exact opposite is true. The navel serves as a reminder that our lives and bodies are gifts from other people. We cannot fail to notice this sign since nature has positioned it in the very center of our bodies. It is a representation of our mothers' goodness, love, and selfless sacrifice. Mothers were viewed by Nagai as representations of grace and God.

According to Nagai, the navel prevents us from becoming overly conceited when things are going well by bringing us back to reality and the fundamentals. When he was taking himself too seriously, he wrote about a helpful lesson he learned. He was in the restroom. He lacked a septic tank and adequate toilet paper, just like the impoverished people around him. Just as he was going to use a piece from the box of torn newspapers, he noticed his own picture looking up at him!

In his hometown of Shimane Prefecture, he drew a pig with a curly tail, which is now the emblem of a confectionery brand. In response to a letter from an A-bomb survivor who was feeling sorry for himself since he was bedridden and "useless," this postcard drawing was created. "Even though we are both suffering from radiation sickness, let's not give up on life, even if we are behind in everything, like the pig's tail," Nagai wrote beneath his illustration of the curly-tailed pig. The tail also has a role to play. After a while, the guy replied, "Thanks to your letter, I am now getting about, trying to play my pig's-tail part in life, with the help of two dogs and a cart."

His two young children were permitted to lie next to their father in Nyokodo on special nights. He was ecstatic one night when he woke up in the wee hours of the morning to the sound of their quiet breathing. We're alive, we're alive!" he wrote with a pencil. And we have an entirely new day ahead of us! He wrote more and more for his two children as he realized his time was running out. He remembers when Makoto was a young boy and courageously attended Grandfather's funeral in lieu of his soldier father. As the melancholy small procession ascended the slope behind the old house with the kaya thatch roof, snow whirled around it. Even though Makoto was only four years old, Midori had written to Nagai about how the young child had blinked the snowflakes from his eyes and accelerated his meager steps to avoid falling behind. "Ascending that snow-covered hill, Makoto," Nagai said, "is a symbol of our current lives in defeated Japan."

"You will soon be orphans and, willy-nilly, must climb a steep, rugged, and lonely path," he writes in a book he composed specifically for them when Makoto was fourteen and Kayano was eight. You cannot use your Christian religion as a painkiller. However, I can promise you that God has specifically selected your lonely route for you in his Providence! Ask him frequently, "How can I use this for your glory?" and accept it as such. There is no clever way to get over the blues, no popular psychology. No, it's the only genuine answer to life's enigma. Accept your happiness as his Providence as well, and in prayer, ask him to protect it for his glory.

"Illness and difficulties do not indicate that we are far from God or that he has turned us away. Examine the lives of notable saints of our day, such as Bernadette of Lourdes and Thérèse of Lisieux. No, we do not believe in a God of insignificant actions who arbitrarily disregards the others while allowing his favorites to win lotteries. He is too wonderful to behave in such a manner. However, genuine prayer will always be answered by him! You frequently witness the recovery of sick persons who know how to pray. That isn't always a miracle.

Living in the midst of his grace and tranquility frequently leads to it naturally. It would be wonderful if my leukemia could be magically cured. It's okay if I'm not cured, and I won't be bothered by it at all. I only care about what he has in store for me; the only life that interests me is one that is lived for him, day by day, with prayer at my side. God has never declared that in order to have lived successfully, you must have done great things for your nation and humanity. What would happen to everyone who is ill in the world? Take my constant need for assistance, for example. You wouldn't claim that the world's bedridden and ill people are "useful"! However, utility isn't the goal. If we continue to live lovingly and accept the circumstances that Providence puts us in with love, our lives are very valuable. When a sick person understands this, their life will be so full that they won't have any space for morbid death wishes.

A bouquet of lotus blooms was given to Nagasaki by some young people from Hiroshima. The lotus has always maintained a special place in Buddhist hearts and is the symbol of Hiroshima. Its ability to grow and blossom amid foul-smelling bogs led to its selection as a representation of the Buddha's compassion, which purges corrupt human hearts of their goodness. The Hiroshima gesture impressed Nagai, who replied with white roses, a Christian emblem, from his Nyokodo garden.

Mary is the perfect example of the rose, which is the Christian emblem of love. "Mystical Rose" was one of her old titles that Nagai adored. "Rosary" is derived from the Latin word "rosarium," which means "rose garden," he pointed out. The Hidden Christians of Nagasaki had made prayer to Mary a central part of their devotion, and Nagai adopted this practice as well. Despite the fact that his first cabin in the wrecked Urakami was nearly empty, he thought it was sufficiently furnished "when it possessed a New Testament, a crucifix, and a statue of Mary," items he kept by his side. A Protestant fundamentalist showed up in Nyokodo shortly before he passed away. The figure of Mary offended the guest, who then harshly criticized Nagai for "heathen worship." When Nagai said, "Wait there now," his smile vanished. He took a moment to make his point clear. "I believe you violate the Bible's teaching on images with your limited interpretation. You adore the man-made, easily idolized images in your own imagination. So much more subdued for seeming spiritual! He continued by drawing on both his personal experience and the experiences of centuries of Christians, arguing that prayer to Mary brings one to the core of the Gospels—that is, becoming a devoted follower of Christ. A tree can be identified by its fruit. The experience of the fruits of the Holy Spirit is brought about by prayer to Mary.

The Hidden Christians used to sing a folk song about the Church eventually returning to Japan "in ships sent by the Holy Father with sails carrying the sign of Mary." The song was coded to be useless to bounty hunters who might overhear it. Archbishop Furstenburg, the Vatican's nuncio to Japan, visited Nyokodo on May 14, 1949, with a Rosary and a message from Pope Pius XII. The song was almost realized, and when Nagai accepted the beads, tears ran down his cheeks. That Rosary remained on his bed until two years later, when he passed away while holding it.

Cherry Blossoms Fall on the Third Day

When Nagai's white blood cell count reached an alarming 390,000 per cubic millimeter in February 1950, his physician concluded that his time was running out. Hajime, his younger brother, gathered the entire family around him. Nagai chose to cheer them up since he was annoyed by how depressed they appeared. Everyone started laughing when he started sharing amusing tales from his army days. According to biographer Kataoka, Nagai's acquaintances regarded this capacity to transcend beyond suffering and exude joy to be highly appealing.

As previously mentioned, Buddhist Japan takes pride in the lengthy tradition of the Nenbutsu, which is the silent recitation of the prayer "Namu Amida Butsu, I depend on you utterly, Amida Buddha," frequently on juzu prayer beads. The widespread use of a form of Christian Nenbutsu, in which Christians condemned to death were tortured to break their spirits, is described in the stories of seventeenth-century Japanese Christians. Others were slashed to poles in frigid water in Sendai, others were slowly burned to death at the Unzen hot springs, and yet others were tied to wooden stakes in Edo (now Tokyo). Like a Nenbutsu, they repeatedly mumbled, "Jesus, Mary, Joseph." In a sort of straightforward prayer of contemplation, "Jesus, Mary Joseph." During the persecutions of the 1860s and 1870s, we read about the same thing occurring. During this final and most agonizing year of his life, Nagai's prayers became increasingly frequent. His temperature would occasionally reach 102 degrees for ten hours at a time. When Makoto or a family member would sneak in to check on Nagai, they would find him facing his altar and repeatedly saying, in a barely discernible whisper, "Jesus, Mary, Joseph."

There was no medication to relieve the discomfort that Nagai's leukemia was now producing, which was accompanied by bone swelling. To his doctor's surprise, however, he was diligently finishing Nyokodo Zuihitsu (Reflections from Nyokodo), a book that many consider to be his best. He would get up with a cup of coffee and start reading his book since he could never sleep past three or four in the morning. His thoughts kept returning to those old pals, the Nagasaki martyrs. Although he has previously written about them, the long and in-depth chapter he gives them in this book drastically alters his writing approach. It appears to be a personal version of the Way of the Cross. He depicts brutality and brutal deaths, as well as God's awful silence and seeming failure. One gets the impression that he is comforting himself as he considers his deteriorating health and the future of his two children by telling his readers that the 26's violent deaths are significant and lovely.

Nagai describes Paul Miki's final hour, one of the twenty-six people who were crucified at Nagasaki, in great detail and with emotion. Living and dying loyal to one's shukun, or liege lord, is the highest virtue according to the samurai's bushido code. Because the cherry blossom's petals fall three days after the flower blooms, samurai picked it as their own insignia. Samurai are expected to be prepared to die young if honor demands it. Like Francis Xavier and his successor, Valignano, Nagai recognized the fantastic aspects of this ideal as well as its inherent perils. Before passing away, Miki sang a "farewell song," and Nagai, who is descended from samurai, decided it was time to write his own. The white rose, not the cherry blossom, served as his inspiration. Naturally, the rhythm of Japanese poetry is impossible to convey in English, but Nagai's verse said, "Good-bye, my flesh." The scent must now depart from the rose, thus I must travel beyond.

Early in 1951, he received news that cheered him up and inspired him to write his final book: the Jesuits were constructing a pilgrim shrine at Otome Tooge, Tsuwano. That was the location of the ice and fire trial for Jinzaburo Moriyama, the father of the priest who baptized Nagai, as well as the horrific deaths of his brother Yujiro, 14, and thirty-five other people for their Christian beliefs. Nagai had discussed this "exile in Babylon" with old Jinzaburo and other survivors on numerous occasions. He had gathered a lot of information and had long planned to publish a book about it, but he suddenly understood that he had to write it now or never. Three days before a severe hemorrhage paralyzed his right arm, on April 22, 1951, he completed the book that he had started on April 1, 1951. Less than a week later, he passed away. Otome Tooge (The Virgin Pass), the name of the mountain pass outside of Tsuwano where Christians were tortured and imprisoned, is the title of Nagai's work. This eighty-one-page book's spiritual and literary appeal played a significant role in Tsuwano's rise to prominence as a popular destination for Christian pilgrims in contemporary Japan. When Nagai's physical and neurological systems were practically shutting down, the doctors who performed the autopsy upon his death were astounded that he had written the book. Because he made so many blunders in his lifelong love, Chinese ideographs, close friends were able to detect the strain. That final bodily anguish was acknowledged by Nagai as fitting for a writer of martyrs. Tertullian, who lived in the third century, is quoted as saying, "The blood of martyrs is the seed of Christians," in the book's final sentence. The final words Nagai wrote were these ones.

In order for the young students to witness the last stages of leukemia, he had instructed Nagasaki University Hospital, his alma mater, to come and pick him up before he passed away. But before he left Nyokodo, there was something he needed to make clear. In a letter, the Italian Association of Catholic Doctors informed him that they had sent him a statue of Our Lady of Peace made of white Carrara marble. They had carried it to Rome in December 1950, where Pius XII consecrated it, before loading it onto the boat for Japan. Inspired by Nagai's writings, they intended that this statue would stand in front of the Nagasaki cathedral, inviting people to pray for peace. Nagai was overjoyed. Together, they determined that the statue should be placed at the southwestern entrance of the cathedral when the administrator visited Nyokodo. Nagai has a sturdy basis built right away by stonemasons. When the statue-carrying ship docked in Kobe in March, the monument mysteriously vanished.

As he waited for the statue of peace in Nyokodo, he animatedly addressed his loved ones, friends, and guests about the importance of working and praying for the prohibition of war, especially nuclear war. "There is an urgent need for a peace movement composed of individuals who are dedicated to justice, tolerance, and love, and who are fired by a commitment that involves personal sacrifice and heart conversion," he stated. We cannot overcome self-centeredness, which is the true enemy of peace, without these.

Nearly all of the time, Nagai was in pain, and his mind kept returning to the Requiem Mass, where he had asked Urakami Christians to view the A-bomb victims as hansai, Holocaust victims to be dedicated to God in faith. Even though he was now a living Hansai, he still had his peace of mind. He claimed that this was firsthand evidence that his Hansai insight was correct.

He thought about agnostics and atheists. He never lost his empathy for them, nor did he forget that he had himself been an atheist. In a somber tone, he said, "A scientist who says we came from the chance mutations of amoeba can't really see rainbows, and that's a great pity." He stated, "We have to keep praying for them." He was still unaware that the end was just a few days away. His doctor knew he was in a lot of agony, and his right arm was now totally paralyzed. But there was no sign of this on Nagai's calm face, and he spent the day in prayer.

On the evening of April 29, he experienced yet another severe bleed, this time in his right thigh, which grew enormously. He could no longer endure the agony in silence, and his family knelt around him, alarmed by his moans and worried that the end was imminent. They carried his sister to his side from a hospital bed. She pleaded with him to "hold on because so many depend on you," after being horrified by his condition. "But it hurts so much," he exclaimed. "Please pray for me, please pray for me. If only He would come soon." After receiving a morphine injection from the doctor, he fell slept for a few hours.

The "child of song," Nurse Utako, remained by his side the entire night. At one in the morning, he woke up upset and extremely thirsty. She said, "I'll get you a drink." "No, I will wait until after that because I want to receive the Eucharist today," he said. "But, Doctor, the fast is not required of sick people." He answered in a cracking voice, "Yes, I know, but I'll wait." He kept asking her the time since he was unable to fall back asleep. "Send my boy Makoto to the cathedral immediately," he remarked when she finally announced that it was five in the morning. By now, Father will be awake. Inform him that I want to partake in the Eucharist.

The priest arrived right away. Nagai bowed with difficulty, listened carefully to the prayers, and then accepted the small consecrated host with another strained bow. He remained motionless until his fifteen minutes of Thanksgiving were over. He was given a drink of water, milk, and crushed strawberries by the nurse. In order to transport him to the hospital, his buddies from the Society of Saint Vincent de Paul then showed up with a wooden stretcher they had constructed. As they hoisted him onto the stretcher, Nagai's lifelong pupil Matsuo-san observed how every shock caused waves of agony to wash over his face. Like Saint Francis when he took a final, loving glance at the town of Assisi and its mountainous surroundings when they brought him inside to die, Nagai closed his eyes, feigning sleep, but outside he opened them and gazed for the final time on Nyokodo with thankfulness and sorrow in his eyes.

Nagai indicated he was ready to go on by bowing to the church. Taking his stretcher's handles, four buddies set off again. Was it the intensity of the sunlight or the emotional surge too much for his frail nervous system? When Matsuo-san noticed a problem, he asked Nagai how he was feeling and motioned for the carriers to halt. "I've lost my vision," he answered. One of them ran off and came back with a bottle of whiskey and everything else he could find! Nagai took a nip, grinned, and acknowledged that the drink might be helpful.

Matron Hisamatsu, an old friend, showed up and escorted them to his room. When Matron Maeda entered, she started to talk upbeatly but broke down when she saw how awful he looked. She attempted to conceal her face with a handkerchief in confusion. "Yes, this is our Matron Maeda, still as genteel as the empress!" Nagai grinned. In spite of themselves, the matrons chuckled. "Do you want to be sponged by us?" Hisamatsu uttered those words. "Yes, please, my entire body." He was requesting that they get his body ready for death, and they understood. Taking a bath before passing away is a Japanese ideal.

Professors and physicians then stopped over, and his family showed up, thrilled to see how much stronger and younger he appeared. When night fell, they gathered around the bed to say evening prayers. They left when the physicians reassured them that there was no imminent threat and advised him to get plenty of rest. Despite a look of sadness on his face, he remained silent. Nurse Utako and his son Makoto made the decision to stay with him. He looked about, confused, and asked where the rest of the family was at 9:40 p.m. after experiencing vertigo due to a brief dizzy spell. His entire body started to tremble, and he muttered in a raspy voice, "Call Shinpu-sama, please." Utako asked Nagai if he wanted any Lourdes water and instructed young Makoto to have someone call the cathedral. He drank it immediately after nodding. He fell unconscious almost instantly, and a doctor who had just entered the room gave him a stimulant injection. In a fruitless attempt to concentrate, Nagai's eyes opened and wandered around. He prayed firmly, "Jesus, Mary, Joseph," but his voice became raspy and they could almost hear him finish, "Into your hands I commend my spirit." Pushing the large family crucifix at Makoto, the astonished Utako gestured to his father, and the child, crying, brought it to the side of the bed. Nagai's right hand now resembled a dying bird's broken wing. His left arm, which had just about managed to support Pius XII's Rosary, suddenly shot upward and grabbed the crucifix out of his son's grasp. "Inotte kudasai," he screamed in a voice so powerful it was shocking. Please, please, pray. All at once, it was over. It was strong and spectacular, yet swift and calm, a dying throe unlike any Matron Hisamatsu had ever witnessed.

The doctor reassured the cathedral priest, who was astonished and felt bad that Nagai had passed away without receiving the final rites: "We were all taken unawares." It was impossible to predict that he would pass away so soon. "I know Dr. Nagai had one worry," the matron continued. His family would be distressed because his ailment typically results in bleeding from all directions when a patient passes away. He passed away so swiftly and quietly, which was a blessing. Accepting this consolation, the priest said, "Today is May 1st, which is Mary's month. I don't believe it's merely a coincidence. I believe she physically visited him in order to bring him to the Lord.

For All That Has Been, Thanks; for All That Will Be, Yes

An extensive autopsy was conducted on May 2 from 1:30 to 5:30 p.m. by a team of physician-officials from ABCC, the Atomic Bomb Casualty Commission, department heads from the university hospital, and doctor-professors. They learned that Nagai passed away from leukemia-related heart failure. A normal spleen weighs roughly 3.3 ounces, but his weighed an astounding 7.52 pounds. He had four and a half times the size of his normal liver. The fact that he had lived so long and finished writing his final two works astounded them.

A sizable group of people, many of them in tears, gathered in a half circle around the hut as friends carried him back to Nyokodo in an unpainted pine coffin. Makoto, who had been raised to be a tough and self-reliant lad by his father, suddenly collapsed over the open casket and sobbed, "See, Daddy, see." See how you were adored by all! In a serious vow to assume Nagai's paternal role, Hajime, Nagai's younger brother, stood beside the coffin alongside Makoto and Kayano and had his picture taken. He was to dutifully keep his pledge, as was his wife, Takako.

Twenty thousand mourners were crammed into and around the Urakami Cathedral on May 3 for the funeral. Archbishop Yamaguchi began the ancient Latin Requiem, which Nagai had adored, with a procession at 9 a.m. Mass on Christmas Eve, 1932, marked the start of Nagai's Christian journey at Urakami Cathedral. It was appropriate that Mass be said here. The mayor of Nagasaki moved forward and bowed down in front of the coffin when the archbishop finished with the absolution. He gently straightened and bowed once more, first to the assembly and then to the archbishop. He read out three hundred sympathy messages solemnly, starting with Prime Minister Yoshida's and concluding with the final one ninety minutes later. The archbishop invited the mayor and Nagai's family to sprinkle holy water on his old friend's coffin. When the clock hands miraculously shifted to 12 noon, the mayor had just given the altar server back the holy water spray. Yamada-san, the buddy who had accompanied Nagai to unearth the same bell on Christmas Eve 1945, rang the Angelus, and it roared loudly. It had been a lone bell that night, but now the city was filled with the sound of bells in Buddhist temples and church steeples.

To the soft notes of In Paradisum, which read, "May angels lead thee into paradise and the martyrs receive thee into Jerusalem, the Holy City," the casket was borne from the cathedral. May angelic choirs welcome you into eternal peace with the once impoverished Lazarus. Before the chief mourners started to move, the front of the procession headed south on foot to the cemetery. The archbishop gazed down with passion at the river of stark black kimonos that were tempered by the Catholic women's white veils. One bystander believed that the sky might nearly burst open and that Beethoven, one of Nagai's heroes, would appear to lead the Eroica Symphony's funeral march!

In a garden plot created and cared for by the city, Dr. Nagai's ashes were interred next to Midori's. It lies just in front of the western entrance to Gaijin Bochi, the "foreigners' cemetery," and only a short stroll from the tram stop in front of the Urakami train station. Dr. Nagai selected the epitaphs on the gravestone from Luke the physician's Gospel. Mary's response to the angel Gabriel is Midori: "I am the Lord's handmaid. Let me be treated in accordance with your promise. Luke 17:10, which reads, "We are unworthy servants; we have only done what was our duty," is his own.

I was looking at these graves with a man I had met the day before, who was quite willing to impart his vast knowledge, thirty-four years later. Despite their never having met, he claimed that Nagai had been his onshi, or esteemed instructor. He clarified: "After the surrender and the American occupation, I was a very angry young man." All of our officials, even our instructors, had assured us that Nippon, the land of the gods, could never be overthrown, and I felt duped and betrayed by them. Both my future and Japan's appeared extremely dismal. I became interested in Nagai after I happened upon one of his works at a public library. Despite being in much worse circumstances than the majority of us, this man exuded optimism. I read more of his novels, and they led me to a decision: either life, human endeavor, and individual principles were ultimately pointless, or there was Nagai's God, who is always good, even though it might not seem so at the moment. I felt that studying Christianity seriously was worthwhile because of something in Nagai's texts. I was baptized and came to share his religion. He was now a science teacher at a high school and frequently traveled to Nagasaki on pilgrimage, visiting the graves of Takashi and Midori Nagai as well as Nyokodo.

Above us, the branches were filtered by the intense Nagasaki sunshine, creating intricate designs at our feet. Light and shade danced like partners in a quadrille as a cool gust of wind blew up from the port, brushing the trees. Sunlight is undoubtedly the most magnificent thing in nature. It is colorless but gives us the appearance of color; it is colorless yet includes all hues. I had gone to a presentation on the perils of nuclear war a few days prior. According to one speaker, plants and consequently humans are kept alive by the process of photosynthesis that sunlight induces in them. "The very process that produces sunlight is used in exploding the H-bomb," he said in a comment that I thought was intriguing. I questioned my scientific acquaintance about if this was a fact or just a theory.

He answered, "It is a scientific fact," and went on to give me a straightforward explanation. A massive mass of compressed hydrogen, with a temperature of fifteen million degrees Celsius, is located at the sun's core. Hydrogen atoms fly with amazing velocity and collide with one another under this heat and pressure. In addition to the tremendous energy released in the form of sunlight, radio waves, microwaves, infrared and ultraviolet rays, gamma and x-rays, and so on, the collision creates new helium atoms. Even though this solar process uses 100 billion tons of hydrogen per day, there is still enough hydrogen to sustain it for millions of years. Without the sun's distance, the earth's atmosphere, and the ozone layer, sunlight would destroy us. The process is known as "atomic fusion" or "nuclear fusion" because the hydrogen atoms in the sun combine to form helium atoms. An initial splitting (fission) of uranium or plutonium atoms produces the pressure and heat required for the fusion in the H-bomb. The atomic fusion of the H-bomb was far more deadly than the nuclear fission-based bombs of Hiroshima and Nagasaki.

Although I had nothing scientific to offer, I did add: "Nagai wrote and spoke extensively on Francis of Assisi. A Franciscan who was stationed in Assisi when I went once made a fantastic statement about the saint that also relates to Dr. Nagai. Francis referred to the sun and wind as his brothers and the moon and water as his sisters in the original draft of The Canticle of the Sun. The Pope then ordered Rome's top physicians to attempt to treat him after he started to go blind. Applying red-hot iron plates to his temples was one of their current extreme tactics! He then included the following passage about fire in his canticle: "Praised be Thou, my Lord, for Brother Fire, by whom Thou lightest the night." He is muscular and strong, and he is gorgeous and happy. In lovely brightness and light rain, it is easy enough to glimpse God. He was seen to Francis and Nagai in every aspect of the cosmos, including the midsummer heat, the autumnal typhoons, the midwinter blizzards, the darkness, and the suffering. I proposed that Francis may add another line of appreciation for Brother Nuclear-Fusion-in-the-Sun if he were still with us today.

"Yes," my Japanese friend said, "maybe! Men like Saint Francis and Nagai were able to perceive nature's otherworldly aspect. Because they only observe the natural, many contemporary poets find it difficult to write life-related rhymes and melodies. The Franciscan vision is cosmic, whereas theirs is only terrestrial. Some of the best poems ever written on romantic love can be found in Japan's ancient Manyoshu poetry, which Nagai loved. However, Nagai realized that the Manyoshu lacks the magical love dimension, which is necessary for romantic love to avoid becoming frustrating or worse. Nagai was able to comprehend Francis's love for Clare—a love that transcends physical manifestation. Thus, when he discovered Midori's burnt skeleton, he was not depressed.

"That's the point of Nagai's parable about the hen that found an egg out in the open," my friend went on. It rested on the motherless egg through all types of weather, giving it all of its warmth and energy to help it hatch out of compassion. Finally, the egg made noises and the shell split open. A duckling appeared! It paddled down to a pond and set out to find its own kind without even saying "thank you." Nagai had a clear understanding that everything, both inside and outside of us, is a gift from God: our loved ones, our abilities and knowledge, our obligations, and life. So we can't ever use other people. We have to be ready to serve and be content with it. Like Francis, Nagai had a deep love for life and the natural world, but he was able to accept their passing in peace because he focused on God, the Source of all real and lovely. The teacher fell silent again after saying that.

I broke the stillness, emboldened by his want to accomplish everything related to Nagai: "Sensei, here we are beside his grave in Nagasaki." Is asking you to sing "The Bells of Nagasaki" too much to ask? That is the song that Yuji Koseki composed and poet Hachiro Sato wrote for the first Nagai film. It has become a staple in Japan and has been likened to Danny Boy in terms of popularity and atmosphere. "Yorokonde," the instructor said with a smile. With pleasure," he said, and his powerful voice soared into the air, startling the nearby doves and sparrows.

Nagai has been likened to the second secretary-general of the United Nations, Dag Hammarksjöld, who passed away in 1961. Both men left behind significant works on peace and a fondness for the sudden and economical evocativeness of haiku poetry. That song about Nagasaki maidens singing as they perished as full burnt offerings may have been penned by Hammarksjöld. In Hammarksjöld's notebook, which was later published as the posthumous book Markings, Nagai may have penned the first line of 1953: "Thanks for everything that has been." Yes, for everything that will be. The two men's harrowing paths from agnosticism and unbelief to a strong confidence in the God of the Bible were likewise similar.

Both survived and perished in the whirlpool of contemporary existence. They wrote intelligently about government, education, science, culture, and peace movements and loved life. Both, however, emphasized the necessity of viewing these issues through the spiritual light that results from individual prayer. The dispersed and garish hues of human experience are collected into the simplicity and clarity of daylight by prayer, which acts as a prism in reverse.

Pascal was the one who introduced Nagai to prayer. There isn't a more appropriate way for me to conclude this Nagai tale than with a well-known quote from Pascal's Pensées. When Nagai initially read it, it confused and disturbed him, but he eventually came to view it as "the one thing necessary."

Copyright © 2025

All rights reserved

The content of this book may not be reproduced, duplicated, or transmitted without the author's or publisher's express written permission. Under no circumstances will the publisher or author be held liable or legally responsible for any damages, reparation, or monetary loss caused by the information contained in this book, whether directly or indirectly.

Legal Notice:

This publication is copyrighted. It is strictly for personal use only. You may not change, distribute, sell, use, quote, or paraphrase any part of this book without the author's or publisher's permission.

Disclaimer Notice:

Please keep in mind that the information in this document is only for educational and entertainment purposes. Every effort has been made to present accurate, up-to-date, reliable, and comprehensive information. There are no express or implied warranties. Readers understand that the author is not providing legal, financial, medical, or professional advice. This book's content was compiled from a variety of sources. Please seek the advice of a licensed professional before attempting any of the techniques described in this book. By reading this document, the reader agrees that the author is not liable for any direct or indirect losses incurred as a result of using the information contained within this document, including, but not limited to, errors, omissions, or inaccuracies.

The contents of this book may not be copied, reproduced or transmitted without the express written permission of the author or publisher. Under no circumstances will the publisher or author be responsible or liable for any damages, compensation or monetary loss arising from the information contained in this book, whether directly or indirectly. .

Disclaimer Notice:

Although the author and publisher have made every effort to ensure the accuracy and completeness of the content, they do not, however, make any representations or warranties as to the accuracy, completeness, or reliability of the content. , suitability or availability of the information, products, services or related graphics contained in the book for any purpose. Readers are solely responsible for their use of the information contained in this book

Every effort has been made to make this book possible. If any omission or error has occurred unintentionally, the author and publisher will be happy to acknowledge it in upcoming versions.

Copyright © 2025

All rights reserved

Printed in Dunstable, United Kingdom